Mackinac Island

Inside, Up Close, and Personal

Dennis O. Cawthorne

Mackinac Island: Inside, Up Close, and Personal © 2014 Dennis O. Cawthorne
ISBN 978-1-933926-45-2

All rights reserved. No part of this book may be reproduced or transmitted in any form by any means, electronic, or mechanical, including photocopying and recording, or by any information storage and retrieval system, except for brief excerpts or by permission of the publisher.

Arbutus Press
Traverse City, Michigan
editor@arbutuspress.com
www.Arbutuspress.com

Photo credits:
Michigan Department of Transportation
Steven Blair
Nancy May
Mackinac Island Tourism Bureau
Grand Hotel
Robert Benjamin
St. Ignace News
Mackinac Island Town Crier
Mackinac Island State Park Commission
Detroit News
Clark Bloswick
Becki Barnwell
Jeff Dupre
Detroit Free Press
Mike Byers
Jeff Potter
Archives of Michigan

Library of Congress Cataloging-in-Publication Data available

CONTENTS

Preface	7	Fire	123
Dawn of an Era	9	The Taxes Ain't Bad	129
Street Man	13	A Taxing Situation	132
Mackinac Island Carriage Tours	19	Governor's Residence	135
Presidential Visits	25	A Mackinac Summer Tradition	141
A Very Special People	33	The State Park Commission	145
Handsome Harry's Pardners' Club	39	Commissioner	151
Speak No Evil	40	Park Directors	157
What's in a Name...or a Number?	42	The Great Lease Wars of 1991-1994	161
Murder	45	Yacht Club	167
Three to Remember	51	Land Theft...and Redemption	170
Moral Re-Armament	59	Wings over Mackinac	175
Chamber of Commerce Manager	69	Whatever Floats Your Boat	179
The City	75	Funding the Park	182
Winter	79	The St. Ignace Connection	187
Legislative Days: All Work and No Play	85	Nurse King's Dream	188
Send in the Clowns	89	Dock Porters	189
Somewhere in Time	91	The Convention and Visitor's Bureau	191
Grand Hotel: The Woodfill Era	94	The Great Ferry Wars of 2010-2014	195
Grand Hotel: The Musser Era	97	Blackout	203
Saying Neigh to the Horseless Carriage	103	The Voice of Mackinac Island	205
If You Build It, They Will Come	109	A Place Like No Other	207
Saloon Keeper	115	Changing Times	209
The Evolving Bar Scene	119	About the Author	216
		Index of Names	217

ACKNOWLEDGMENTS

A special thank you to the following who assisted in making this book possible:

Susan Bays
Natasha Oxender
Nate Love
Amanda Chmielewski
Mary McGuire Slevin
Phil Porter
Wes Maurer Jr.
Kelsey Schnell

And especially,
Cynthia Cawthorne
Brevin Cawthorne
Chase Cawthorne

If I omitted anyone from the above listing, it was inadvertent and I thank you, too.

Mackinac Island

A limestone outcropping eight miles in circumference and rising to a height of over 300 feet in the waters where Lake Huron and Lake Michigan meet between Michigan's upper and lower peninsulas; a place of winding shores, towering cliffs, and green forests appearing to Native Americans as a great turtle coming up from the lake, thus the Odawa name, "Michilimackinac."

Rock Fever

-n. a proper noun well-known and often used by native Mackinac Islanders meaning an intense longing, desire, or compulsion to return to Mackinac Island and immerse oneself in everything Mackinac, particularly after having once been there and coming to know not only its physical beauty but also its inhabitants, their foibles and endearing idiosyncrasies; conversely, in the deepest darkest days of winter isolation, an urgent desire or need by locals to flee the Island for a brief respite in more hospitable climes.

PREFACE

Many books have been written about Mackinac Island, usually focusing on its history, its scenic beauty, or its architecture. This is not one of those books. Rather, this book is a nostalgic and candid behind the scenes look at more than a century of Mackinac people and events. It's part memoir, part history, and part chronicle. All of it is true.

Mackinac Island is very much a small town, yet each year it hosts over three quarters of a million people and is often the focal point of national and even international media coverage. It attracts celebrities of every kind as well as masses of "average Americans." It is the summer home of Michigan's governor, frequently a hotbed of state political activity, and a place endlessly fascinating to those who know it.

For a half century and more, beginning in 1960, I came to know and experience Mackinac intimately. I did so through the prism of the many roles I played there during those years: carriage driver, chamber of commerce manager, state legislator, saloonkeeper, attorney, legislative advocate and for over 20 years member and chairman of the Mackinac Island State Park Commission which governs 83% of the Island's land area. Along the way, I built a home, became engaged, got married, and raised two sons there. Probably I will be buried there.

I have been an eyewitness to—and too often involved in—a host of events that one does not normally associate with Mackinac: murder, political intrigue, a disastrous fire, scandal, controversy, hilarity, and high jinks of all kinds, made all the more fascinating by the very fact they happened on Mackinac.

Through it all, I came to know intimately and appreciate Mackinac's rich stew of colorful characters and events, its multiple layers unseen and unknown to casual visitors. But I have not been a passive observer of Mackinac. I like to think I also played a role in shaping and impacting the Mackinac Island of today, I hope for the better.

Designed for those who really want to "know" Mackinac from the inside, this is the story of an amazing half century of life and times on an incredible island.

The official opening of the Mackinac Bridge on November 1, 1958 heralded a new era in Mackinac Island's and all of Northern Michigan's tourism industry. Shown above, (L-R) State Highway Commissioner John C. Mackie; bridge designer David Steinman; Gov. G. Mennen Williams; former U.S. Senator Prentiss M. Brown, chairman of the Mackinac Bridge Authority; former Gov. Murray D. (Pat) VanWagoner, George Osborn, and William Cochran, Authority members; and Larry Rubin, executive secretary of the Authority. Williams, Brown, and VanWagoner all would figure prominently in Island events of the following years.

Dawn of an Era

In June 1960 famed and spectacularly beautiful Mackinac Island, tucked between Michigan's upper and lower peninsula, stood poised for entry into a new era of tourism-based prosperity.

The fur trade, then fishing, and finally tourism had been the engine of past prosperity. The Great Depression with its hard times, and World War II with its gas rationing and travel restrictions, had devastated Mackinac's economy for a quarter century. By the mid-1950s recovery was clearly underway. For the first time, millions of middle class Americans were on the move: for the men and women who worked in southern Michigan's auto and auto-related industries, indeed throughout the Great Lakes region, jobs were plentiful, the pay good, and paid holidays increasingly the norm. A summer vacation "up North" was no longer a luxury of the few.

And now in 1960, within just a two-and-a-half year time span, an array of events had occurred that would open the floodgates of travel and leisure on Mackinac Island. It would be based not on limited numbers of the wealthy travelling on large steamships plying the Great Lakes as in the past. It would involve masses of middle-class Americans travelling by automobile from the great cities and suburbs over I-75, the new four lane expressway now nearly compete and linking the country by a single road from Miami to Mackinac. Many would cross the Straits of Mackinac over the also new five-mile bridge, a tourist attraction in itself, that linked a state previously connected only by slow ferries carrying limited numbers of vehicles. For the first time ever Mackinac was easily and quickly accessible from metropolitan centers for a week or even a single weekend getaway. A new prosperous era of tourism was at hand.

On Mackinac Island itself, historic Fort Mackinac had just been totally refurbished and turned into a major destination attracting thousands to its displays and re-enactments. The exciting young Democratic candidate for President of the United States, John Fitzgerald Kennedy, had just visited the Island, and two days later one of the nation's leading magazines, the *Saturday Evening Post,* featured a major story on W. Stewart Woodfill and the Island's iconic Grand Hotel, producing a public relations bonanza unprecedented in Mackinac history.

That was the year I came to Mackinac Island. I had come to work for the summer between my sophomore and junior year of college. In a sense, I have never left. I had contracted Rock Fever.

The November 1959 opening of the Mackinac Bridge linking I-75 in Mackinaw City to St. Ignace and I-75 in the Upper Peninsula literally paved the way to a tourism boom for Mackinac Island and all of northern Michigan.

John F. Kennedy's visit in June 1960 would bring national media coverage to Mackinac Island. Above, Kennedy comes up the Arnold Line dock accompanied by Democratic leader Neil Staebler, Gov. G. Mennen Williams, and a throng of excited tourists.

The three-man local police force, supplemented in the summer by two state police officers, stands guard not long before I first came to the Island in the summer of 1960. Flanked by state troopers are locals (L-R) Ozro Smith, Otto (Bud) Emmons, and Myron (Junior) Bloomfield. In later years the force grew to much larger numbers, often recruited from off the Island, and at times criticized for being over-zealous.

Street Man: My Introduction to Mackinac

I had never set foot on Mackinac Island before I came to work there as a college student on June 22, 1960. "Too expensive," my mother would say the two or three times we left our home in Manistee, Michigan to ride the ferries that then linked the state's two peninsulas on a route a few miles west of the Island.

My Albion College fraternity brother, Bob Roe, had worked there in the summers of 1958 and 1959 for Mackinac Island Carriage Tours, Inc., the company that dominated Mackinac's horse and buggy trade. He had been the first collegian ever hired by the company. The experiment had worked well and the company was looking for more like him in anticipation of the 1960 season. It was a great place to work, Bob assured me, and the company treated its employees well. Besides, with hundreds of other college kids working and partying on the Island, a very good time seemed a certainty.

Bob recommended I apply for the job of carriage tour driver. It was a natural for a history major, he said, and his description of fat tips from satisfied riders only whetted my enthusiasm. I pictured myself driving a spirited yet obedient team of horses, waxing eloquent and providing a narrative of Mackinac lore and legend to passengers eager to hear my every word. I envisioned reaching under my "driver's seat" to extract pieces of candy to hand the youngest tour-takers, the better to soften the hearts of appreciative parents who would be doing the tipping. Lucrative good times were just around the corner.

Unfortunately, I hadn't counted on a day that started at 6 a.m. (I was always a hard worker, but early mornings were never part of my repertoire). Nor had I counted on mucking out manure-covered stable floors, sticking bits into recalcitrant slobbering equine mouths, brushing hair off huge sweaty bodies, or throwing harnesses on and off animals mainly interested in kicking human shins and stomping human feet.

The company and I, by mutual agreement, soon concluded that we were both better served by my being "on the street" holding down one of the positions that entailed procuring tour customers and then loading them on to one of the company's 55 twelve-passenger rigs. Also better, I mentally noted, were the hours of the job, mine being 10 a.m. to 7 p.m. with a two-hour break in the mid-afternoon. And on the street, I discovered, I could get to know the people who ran the company, banter with customers in the waiting line, and interact with the many Island business people who daily walked by the loading zone. For a "people person" with political inclinations it seemed, all in all, the perfect fit.

Carriage Tours, my new employer, was essentially two operations, one the tour, the other a 24 hour taxi service. My immediate supervisor was Jack Chambers, 34-year-old assistant manager of MICT. The company's tour rigs were driven by an array of older, if not old, men who tended to be retired from other jobs, ex-farmers who had grown up around horses, or men otherwise down on their luck. Among them were Mark Hammond, a retired Detroit cop; R. J. "Bob" Smith, a one-legged ex-prize fighter; Hobart Ames, taciturn, dapper, and school-teacherish; Charles Tremethick ("Tamarack"), injured in and ultimately laid off from an Upper Peninsula iron mine; John McMillin whose farm near West Branch could no longer support him; Orvin Christiansen, a shy Yooper whose stuttering provided an added dimension to his tour; and a younger man known only as "Michigan Slim," who drifted South each year when the Mackinac summer gave way to autumn.

Our street crew, my co-workers in the carriage loading zone, were no less unique: Louie Roussin, imperious, moustached, dressed in a uniform that set him off from the rest of us, and looking much too important to be a mere carriage loader; James Dunleavy "Dun" Flanagan, elderly, cherubic, white-maned, the very embodiment of a kindly, mirthful Irishman; Jay Gillespie, handsome and easygoing who, at 30, had opted for permanent street duty after a carriage he was driving plunged part way down a West Bluff cliff, killing the horse and he himself only narrowly escaping; and Willard Lasley, from an old French-Indian Island family, his body wracked by tuberculosis and perhaps too much alcohol, possessed of a mellifluous voice and a rightful pride in being an expert in local history.

There were, in practice, gradations of "street men." I was at the low end. My first job was essentially to stand in the street bawling out to passing pedestrians the virtues of the one and a half hour guided tour and answering the inevitable questions tourists asked in response to my ministrations. The next grade up, to which I fortunately ascended, was that of a sort of a passenger processor.

I soon learned that loading a tour carriage was not simply a matter of boarding passengers according to their place in line. There was, instead, a mixture of art and science

Albion College students working on the Island in the summer of 1961. Most were employed by Carriage Tours but two, James Kingsley and Michael Harrison, seated in the rear, worked for Grand Hotel and went on to distinguished careers as judges.

involved. Each of the three rows in a carriage had four seats. It was simple enough to load a family or group of four average-sized persons. Since it was essential to fill every seat, for economy reasons, things began to get complicated if there was only one in the party, or if one or more in the party were of such girth that they would take up more than the allotted "average size" seat. For reasons unknown, we code-named the latter a "Colorado." One "Colorado" and a small child would therefore be equal to two spaces, and we planned accordingly.

Some groups would refuse to be split up. Complicating matters children had to be placed in seats in the middle of the row. Weights had to be evenly distributed. Older people were best placed in the front near the driver, the better to hear, and, this being 1960, people of color loaded at the last possible moment and preferably in the back row so as to not provoke an already seated Caucasian to "jump ship." Covertly eyeing persons in the waiting line, we would do a quick mental inventory of body size, weights, color, and ages in order to properly configure a contented and perfectly arranged load. If kids were whining or we sensed people unhappy with being packed too close together, we would dispatch a load with astonishing speed. If a carriage lingered late in the day only partially loaded we would hold it at bay, praying for more passengers until we discerned that the suffering patrons already on board would tolerate delay not a second longer. Some days we dispatched over 230 loads carrying nearly 2,500 passengers. In all, it was a real education, not all of it pretty.

The horse-drawn taxis, lined up across the street from the tours, required more skill to operate and a detailed knowledge of local destinations. They were driven almost exclusively by locals: two young men in their mid-20s, Dennis Dufina, with movie-star looks, and Ducky Smith, dark and solidly built; young George Wellington, bespectacled son of long-time Island school superintendent Charles Wellington; bushy browed, impish Chester O'Brien, a cigar perpetually extending from a toothless mouth; and Phil ("Weenix") Cadreau, a genial, slightly overweight French-Indian who, tarrying too long once at a local saloon while on taxi duty, emerged to find that his team had been unhitched from his rig, then turned around, put back in their traces and re-hitched so that the horses' rumps were forward and their heads faced into the dinky seat. (Cadreau, it was said, swore off drinking for the next six months.) Street boss and dispatcher for the taxi operations was Les O'Brien, a 60-ish former mayor and proud Irishman.

Everyday on the main street, near our carriage loading zone, there passed by some of the colorful Island business proprietors I got to know that first summer: big, slow-moving Amos Horn of Horn's Palm Café; his brother, quick, wiry Ty Horn, owner of Ty's Lunch, who enjoyed striding through his restaurant with a toilet plunger over his shoulder, telling customers he was headed to the kitchen to stir the soup; Iggy Palermo, the very Italian proprietor of the Chatterbox Restaurant operated by him, his wife Catherine and their eight children, and whose female employees we college guys called "Iggy's Little Piggies;" Dennis Brodeur, a self-effacing World War II naval pilot who later flew mail to the Island in wintertime and now operated the Wandrie Restaurant; and finally, Harry Stamas, known to all as "Harry the Greek," whose Astor Café stood opposite the Thunderbird Gift Shop, operated by Egyptian Roben Arbib, the two—each in heavily-accented broken English—shouting and insulting each other in mid-street in verbal confrontations they both obviously enjoyed.

I had one day off from work all summer, but somehow it didn't seem to matter: the social life more than made up for it. The Island employs hundreds of summer workers, in the late 1960s consisting mainly of college students, a majority of them fetching young females chosen as much for their good looks and pulchritude as for their waitressing, bartending, or housekeeping skills. Party time was most of the time. Beer was the vice of choice, narcotics being practically unknown at that time at least in the upper Midwest. Even though many of the college kids hadn't reached the legal drinking age of 21, the new carriage loader included, there prevailed on the Island a general live-and-let-live attitude. The Island's many bars "carded" only sporadically – the Island's deputy sheriff bought me my first under-age drink – and the taps flowed freely at moonlit beach and bonfire keg parties. When the local cops on duty did stop by at the beach parties, it was often to share in the bounty themselves, and I cannot recall a single kid ever being carded there much less ticketed and arrested as a minor in possession.

Beyond all the good times that summer on one of the world's most beautiful resort destinations, there was this: the faint aroma of political machinations, the brooding omnipresence of something called Moral Re-Armament, an unsolved murder in our midst, and local characters more colorful than I had ever met elsewhere. Mackinac was a place unlike any other this twenty-year-old had yet experienced.

My first Mackinac summer came to an end on Labor Day 1960. While I had thoroughly enjoyed the Island, I decided to do something different the next summer.

And so I did. I was employed as a relief police officer in my hometown of Manistee, Michigan, working midnights ten days on, four days off. At the dawn of each first day off, I found myself in the car and heading 185 miles north to Mackinac. I couldn't stay away.

I couldn't resist getting co-workers of mine from 1960, Chester O'Brien (L) and J.D. "Dun" Flanagan (R), both of Carriage Tours, to pose with me under this sign welcoming attendees at the 1965 National Governors Conference.

Mayor Arthur T. Chambers, future leader of Mackinac Island Carriage Tours, is introduced to Gov. Murray D. (Pat) VanWagoner in 1941 by the ubiquitous Wilfird Doyle. VanWagoner had recently appointed Doyle to another term on the State Park Commission this time in the capacity of the newly-minted title of "resident commissioner." Under the law then (but not now) resident commissioners were appointed by the governor upon recommendation of the City's mayor. Two decades later I would come to know all three gentlemen.

Mackinac Island Carriage Tours

Mackinac Island Carriage Tours, Inc. ("Carriage Tours"), the company for which I had gone to work, was the creature of a 1948 consolidation forced by the Mackinac Island State Park Commission. Prior to that time, dozens of independent rig owners plied Mackinac's streets and wharves in a ferocious, sometimes unscrupulous, competition for tourist dollars. There were no standards and no rules. Carriages were of various sizes, shapes, and colors, safety features often lacking. Hack drivers dressed in whatever garb pleased them on a particular day. Prices were negotiable and subject to haggling and undercutting. Routes, and the stories told on them, varied greatly in quality and authenticity. It was all cut-throat free enterprise practiced in the extreme. Moreover, the image projected to Island visitors was often negative and good for neither the customer nor the service provider. Some of the leading carriage men agreed with the Commission that change was necessary and the worst abuses in need of fixing. In 1948, after many fits and starts, a new consolidated company was born.

The system put in place essentially required carriage owners to lease their family-owned carriage licenses to a new company with centralized management and with them as shareholders. Now there were to be standard uniforms, fixed prices, established routes, approved tour texts and, most importantly, one centrally-supplied source, style, and color of safe carriages. The horses themselves would no longer be stabled in various places around town but instead in a new large barn in Harrisonville.

A few operators, notably Taylor Gough and his son Jack, as well as Jack Chambers, successfully resisted inclusion but virtually everyone else eventually capitulated to the new enterprise that would be under the strict supervision of the State Park Commission. (Up to the present day, the Gough taxis are owned and operated separately from Carriage Tours and are differentiated by their blue and yellow color scheme.)

One of the by-products of the consolidation, as I soon learned first hand, was that virtually all of the stockholders held some kind of paid job with the company regardless of whether the company really needed them or the work they provided. That, plus the wide

These Albion College students, among the first collegians ever to be hired as drivers by Carriage Tours, Inc., pose in 1961 in front of Horn's Palm Café with F. Dudleigh Vernor, composer of the famous "The Sweetheart of Sigma Chi." Front (L-R), Tom Megdall, Jim Hansz, Bob Fischer, Mike Vorce, Vernor, Lynn Albee, Jim Cooley, and Hal Rice. Driving the team is Charlie Moore, the college student recruited by Jack Chambers to covertly supply text for the anti-Moral Re-Armament screed, *The Word*. Note at top right the incongruous palm tree, Horn's logo in the early 1960s.

diffusion of ownership, made for a not altogether efficient operation though by any measure a vast improvement over the old one.

The first president of the male-dominated corporation, still in office when I came to work in 1960, was—astonishing in those days—a female. Mary Franks was a tough South Carolina-born ex-night club manager married to John Franks from an old Island family. The company treasurer was another old independent operator, Carl Couchois, an elderly bachelor known also for rendering tuba solos at Sunday Mass. General manager of the company, and in fact its real leader and boss was Arthur T. Chambers, long-time carriageman and brother-in-law of John Franks.

When I arrived in 1960, barn operations were ably headed by Jim Chambers, one of Arthur's three sons, and Robert Gillespie, son of a former independent, an Irish Orangeman and Protestant to boot. New carriages were built in company shops supervised by Bud Chambers, another of Art's sons. Battles with the State Park Commission were frequent, usually involving quality of service and the Park's need to get more people off the tour buggies and into the newly refurbished Fort.

When Art Chambers passed away in 1972, his son Bill, a doctor of veterinary medicine, gave up a successful practice in Minneapolis—St. Paul, Minnesota, to return to the Island to literally pick up the company reins. Dr. William K. Chambers was exactly what the company needed. With his brother Jim, Bill began slowly acquiring many of the leased licenses still owned by Island families, carefully pruning unproductive shareholder-employees and consolidating stock ownership. The company sought efficiencies through use of 3-horse hitches for part of the tour, added adjunct businesses, and expanded operations to include the Island dray services which heretofore had been notoriously inefficient and unreliable.

Brad, Dr. Bill, and Jim Chambers, shown here in the summer of 2012, carried on the family tradition at Mackinac Island Carriage Tours. Under their leadership the company came a long way from its 1948 roots and forced consolidation.

Years later, under my chairmanship of the State Park Commission, we minimized our interference in company affairs and trusted the new company leadership to do what was right for the Island and the travelling public, this after four decades of intermittent friction between company and Commission. What I, and perhaps too few others, understood and appreciated was the difficulty of sustaining through turbulent economic times a company that too often was at the mercy of unsteady and usually escalating feed prices, high labor and insurance costs, expensive hard-to-find equipment, the vicissitudes of Michigan weather and, in general, the unique challenges of operating in the 21st century an essentially 19th century business. With the assistance of his son Bradley, Chambers built and strengthened a company absolutely vital to the image and economic well-being of Mackinac. Without horses, Mackinac would be in many respects just another island. Without the Chambers, it could have been without the business that, together with Grand Hotel, symbolizes and is the very essence of Mackinac Island itself.

With Carriage Tours driver Eddie Cadotte, 1965, one of 17 children born to Islanders Fred ("Gunny") and Elizabeth Cadotte.

Dick Gimmel, Carriage Tours blacksmith and ferrier, needed a liquid boost before his starring role on *Today Show's* 1964 telecast.

Agnes Shine was a familiar face in Carriage Tours' taxi office as night dispatcher. Born in Scotland and possessed of a thick and endearing Scottish brogue, Mrs. Shine's residence on historic Market Street was home to numerous Carriage Tour employees, including me, during the summer of 1960.

Former mayor Les O'Brien holds a sign welcoming John F. Kennedy to "the Irish Island of Mackinac," June 1960. W. Stewart Woodfill is at left.

Presidential Visits

Islanders, especially its many staunch Irish Catholic Democrats, were still basking in the afterglow of John F. Kennedy's visit to Mackinac when I first came to Mackinac a few short weeks later in June 1960. Presidential candidate Kennedy had come at the invitation of Governor G. Mennen Williams who himself had briefly pursued his party's nomination. The visit was not about fudge or the lovely scenery. Rather, its purpose was to nail down for Kennedy the Michigan Democratic convention delegates who until that point had been pledged to Williams.

By late May, however, it was clear that Kennedy was the almost certain nominee and some feared that unless Williams and Michigan Democrats moved quickly they would be irrelevant at the July national convention. Donald Thurber, a friend of both Williams and Kennedy and a Harvard Law grad who I came to know many years later, arranged the meeting, though it was Williams who picked Mackinac Island as the site.

On June 2, 1960, Kennedy flew into Pellston Airport, was greeted by Gov. Williams and his wife Nancy, and whisked across the Mackinac Bridge to a waiting Arnold Line ferry. On the Island, the entourage was transported by carriage to the Governor's Residence. Arriving there, Kennedy and Michigan Democratic leaders met around a large table in the dining room while a half dozen reporters huddled on the windswept porch "shivering and drinking coffee" on an unusually cold late spring afternoon.

Emerging from the residence Williams told reporters he was formally endorsing Kennedy, and the last doubt about the inevitability of the Kennedy nomination evaporated. When Kennedy was elected in the subsequent November general election, his first announced appointment was of Williams to be Assistant Secretary of State for African Affairs.

This was not the first nor the last time that a President, ex-President, or would-be President visited Mackinac Island. In the 1920s Mrs. Alvin Hert, owner of what is now the Stonecliffe Mansion, in her role as a member of the Republican National Committee tried to lure President Calvin Coolidge into making Mackinac the "summer White House." In the 1930s, Islanders issued a very public invitation to President Franklin D. Roosevelt to come to Mackinac for a summer retreat. Neither inducement attracted a President, however.

In 1955 ex-President Harry S. Truman came to the Island as a guest of W. Stewart Woodfill, owner of Grand Hotel. Truman's visit gave rise to an episode long-remembered on the Island and still much talked about when I arrived on the Island in 1960. A receiving line for Truman had been arranged for his arrival on the Arnold Line dock, with the stately, urbane Woodfill at its head and Island mayor John R. (Jack) Gough (pronounced Goff) next to him. As Truman reached Gough, the short, stout, ruddy-faced mayor stuck out his hand and, running his two names together, barked out, "Mr. President, JackGough, JackGough." A startled Woodfill turned and in a loud stage whisper to the mayor hissed, "It's John R. Gough, Goddammit, John R. Gough," and stomped his omni-present walking stick on the little stable owner's right foot.

In later years, many more Presidents, would-be Presidents, and ex-Presidents would visit the Island. President Gerald Ford's arrival in July 1975, featuring his return to Fort Mackinac where he had been an Eagle Scout in 1929, caused the biggest stir, in part because it occured at the height of a very busy tourist season. Ford and the First Lady stopped at shops on Main Street, attended services at Trinity Episcopal Church, and enjoyed an overnight at the Governor's Residence. The presidential limousine, ferried to the British Landing dock under the cover of darkness, was discretely hidden away in an MISPC barn, at the ready should any emergency arise. George H. W. Bush came to the 1979 Mackinac Republican Conference and again as an ex-President in the mid-1990s. Bill Clinton, pre-presidency, and Michael Dukakis, at a Democratic Leadership outing at Fort Mackinac hosted by Governor James Blanchard, also visited. Republican nominee John McCain came to the Island and made a stop at the Village Inn in 2007. Mitt Romney, who proposed to his future wife under the Mackinac Bridge, spent time on the Island when his father was governor, and he returned to Mackinac in 2007 and 2011 as a presidential contender.

First ladies also made their appearances in my time. Lady Bird Johnson was a visitor in 1964 and Hillary Clinton came twice, once before her husband became president.

Locals were still talking about former President Harry S. Truman's 1955 visit when I first came to the Island. Welcoming Truman is (L-R) Otto W. Lang and Hugh Rudolph, both of Arnold Transit, and Gov. G. Mennen Williams. A few minutes before, Grand Hotel owner W. Stewart Woodfill "corrected" Island mayor Jack Gough's self-introduction to the ex-Chief Executive.

Presidential spouse Lady Bird Johnson tours Fort Mackinac, summer of 1964, escorted by Park Superintendent Carl Nordberg and State Park Commission Chairman W. Stewart Woodfill. Dr. Eugene Petersen, then Director of Historic Projects, is behind Woodfill.

President and Mrs. Gerald Ford leave services at Trinity Episcopal Church, July 1975. To the right of the Fords, Rev. Roland Raham, his wife, and Lay Reader Marshall Lowell. Behind the presidential couple, Gov. and Mrs. William Milliken, their son Bill, and Marge Griffin, wife of U.S. Senator Robert P. Griffin.

President George H. W. Bush shares a laugh with (L-R) Gov. John Engler, Charlie Williams, long-time Grand Hotel *maitre'd*, and John Hulett, Grand Hotel's vice-president.

Grand Hotel's Dan Musser Jr. welcomes Arkansas Gov. Bill Clinton and wife Hillary to Mackinac. A few years later, Clinton would become the nation's 42nd president. Hillary would return to Mackinac later as First Lady.

Donald "The Duck" Andress, Island resident and proud member of the Sault Ste. Marie Tribe of Odawa Indians, leads a Lilac Day parade.

A Very Special People

What intrigued me most about Mackinac during that first summer of 1960 was the local people I met and came to know. Summer cottager Bart Huthwaite expressed it well: "Mackinac Island breeds the most interesting, cantankerous, curious, brazen, strange, likable manhood and womanhood known to Western Man and maybe beyond. This eight mile around island boasts a cast of characters that would make even Charles Dickens, that great Victorian chronicler of nineteenth century characters, green with envy . . . These are not characters you see in every day suburban America."

Louie the Thief, Harry the Greek, Handsome Harry, Eagle Eye, Yunk Yunk, and The Duck were just some of the unforgettable characters who crossed my path. Over the years there have been literally hundreds more, most bearing unique nicknames in an Island tradition that goes back generations. (Where else would a succession of local police chiefs in the 1940s thru the early 1960s bear the names "Stringbean," "Hambone," "Junior," and "Boston Blackie"?)

Why Mackinac breeds such individuals has often been a subject of speculation. Some say Mackinac, being a remote trading center in the New World, always attracted rugged, unique characters. Others say a major reason is the Island's winter isolation which, pre-snowmobile, was much greater than it is today. For four winter months with outside influences dwindling to a trickle, Island "character-hood" grows, isolated and unbothered. Still others say the Island's slow pace, especially in pre-television days, allowed the art of bar room story-telling to develop to a high gloss, placing a premium on people and events that infused those stories with zest and color. Whatever the reason, in Huthwaite's words, "Mackinac's people have retained a quaintness and individualism . . . (that most) . . . other communities lost long ago."

But, in addition to the locals, the Mackinac community in summer is comprised of business owners who spend their winters elsewhere, cottage owners who come for four months of favorable weather, and a small army of employees and laborers who service the

Island's three quarters of a million visitors. Thrown together on one small island, these disparate groups blend into a remarkable social melting pot, a place where the usual distinctions based on age, wealth, occupation, family pedigree and socio-economic status somehow end up being irrelevant: at bars, parties, and on the golf course, street sweepers rub elbows with millionaires and college kids hang with people their grandparents' age.

One of my best memories is from early summer of 1967 when I was part of an impromptu mini booze cruise originating in the island harbor. The crew and passengers, in its entirety, consisted of: former Michigan Governor Murray (Pat) VanWagoner, an itinerant piano player, a Catholic priest, two local Indian lads, a college student bartender, a young state legislator, and the boat's owner (whose identity I do not recall). To me, that nautical adventure encapsulated everything I came to like about Mackinac.

A friend once speculated that this social leveling was due at least in part to the fact that everyone on this auto-less island has little choice but to peddle his or her bike to wherever they're going. The puffing, panting, and wheezing as they go up (and down) the Island's steep hills in all kinds of weather somehow produces a common bond, a feeling of "I'm no better than you" and "we're all in this together." Maybe my friend was on to something.

Occupational roles on the Island tended to be fluid and interchangeable, though perhaps less so today than when I first came to Mackinac. In those days I was fascinated by the fact that a local who was a city cop yesterday might be employed as a taxi driver today, a hotel desk clerk tomorrow, and a house painter a month from now. A local Catholic priest occasionally entertained on the accordion at night in the Mustang Lounge and the robed deacon from Trinity Episcopal Church sometimes tended bar at the same establishment. It often seemed as if on Mackinac all the conventions of the outside world were turned upside down but in a quiet, almost endearing, way.

I discovered very early that to really understand and appreciate the Island, it helped to know the history of its local population. The very core and essence of the Mackinac Island community was and is its people of French-Indian heritage and Irish heritage. Native Americans, in particular the Odawas, were of course on Mackinac long before any white man. To them, Mackinac was sacred, the Great Turtle arising out of the inland seas, the dwelling place of the great spirits. When French traders and explorers came to the Straits of Mackinac in the late 1600s, they wasted little time consorting with, marrying, and procreating with the Natives. (Why the English, also present, did not also do so is something I never quite understood.) The inevitable result was a large and growing French-Indian population that tended to move back and forth between the Island and St. Ignace.

In the mid-1990s an eclectic group of Islanders gathered for dinner at the Major's Quarters, next to Fort Mackinac. Nearly all would play a prominent role in the life and times of Mackinac in the latter half of the 20th century. Clockwise beginning at the far right: Mayor Margaret Doud, Dennis Brodeur, Ron Dufina, Bill Chambers, Sue Chambers, Rena Callewaert, Vic Callewaert (standing), Sean , Mary Callewaert, Todd Callewaert, Jen Callewaert, Brad Chambers, Nancy Chambers, Sandra Orr, Dennis Cawthorne, Cynthia Cawthorne, Debra Orr, Jack Chambers, Patti Garrett, and unidentified.

The author with Louie "The Thief" Deroshia, colorful Island businessman of the 1970s and 1980s. When asked if it was true that the burgers sold at his Horse and Buggy Drive Inn were made from horsemeat, he had a one word response: "Neigh." Originally a used car salesman, for a short time he was co-owner of the Mustang Lounge and gave it that Island-appropriate name in part because he was then selling new Fords (including the Mustang model) as a sideline.

The region, and particularly the Island, thus came to be populated by a large number of dark-haired, dark-eyed, often copper-complected people with French names: Cadotte, Cadreau, St. Onge, Bazinaw, Perault, Visnaw, LaPine, Therrien, and more. Families tended to be prolific. One Island family in 1960 had 17 children, another 15. Their homes were clustered in Harrisonville, not a town, but a neighborhood of the Island, in the middle and on its highest ground. If someone was said to live "in the village" it meant they lived in Harrisonville, a place separate and distinct from the downtown or other populated areas of Mackinac. The U.S. government itself had set aside the area in the 1880s during the presidency of Benjamin Harrison and intended it not as an official reservation but—by unspoken understanding—a place for the local French-Indian population to live outside of the Fort and federal park land, and this it was when I arrived in 1960.

The Irish had come to Mackinac in the late 1840s and early 1850s as a direct result of Ireland's potato famine. One of the earliest arrivals was Charles O'Malley whose letters back to Ireland enticed a number of his countrymen to make the Atlantic crossing. Among the early Irish immigrants were the Doud, Chambers, Donnelly, Flanagan, Corrigan, and Murray families. "Charlie" O'Malley went on to serve in the Michigan legislature and build the Island House hotel. As a legislator, he convinced his colleagues to change a number of northern Michigan counties originally having Indian names to names of counties in his native Ireland. Thus came to be the Michigan counties named Wexford, Antrim, Clare, Emmet, and Roscommon.

When I arrived on Mackinac over 100 years later, those families and their descendents were still in residence on the Island, in fact the very embodiment of its social, political, and economic fabric. Their customs, traditions, likes, and prejudices remained very much in evidence. Social mobility and geographic fluidity may have been the norm elsewhere in 20th century America, but the French-Indians and Irish of Mackinac remained rooted, comfortable in their Mackinac surroundings and faithful in many ways to the customs of their ancestors who had settled generations before. When John F. Kennedy made his 1960 visit the local Irish pride swelled over.

Many distinctive local characteristics have not changed over the years. The place still has probably the highest number of nicknames per capita ratio of any place in the country. In my early years, from Harrisonville alone, there hailed the aforementioned Yunk Yunk and Eagle Eye as well as Beaver, Fats, Snapper, Porky, Skeezix, Weenix, Gunny, Cornflakes, Bam Bam, and countless more. Among the feminine gender there were Bag Lady, Ugga Bugga, Squaw, High Pockets, Googie, and Olive Oil. The *Town Crier* ran a contest in the mid-1990s that produced over 400 recognized local nicknames. Not bad considering the previous U.S.

census had recorded a permanent population of almost the exact same number.

Funeral wakes, where the body of the deceased is brought into the family home for viewing, have disappeared practically everywhere else in the country. They still occasionally occur on Mackinac. Some, fueled by mourners who tarried too long at a downtown bar before arriving on the scene, have taken on legendary proportions. One reportedly featured the deceased being removed from the casket and propped up in a sitting position in a corner, beer in hand (unverified). At another, one of the mourners came in from the outside cold, placed a twelve-pack of beer on the casket, proceeded to rip it open and toss the cans one-by-one to the outstretched hands of thirsty co-mourners (verified).

Doud's, the oldest family owned grocery store in the country, still allows its customers to charge their food purchases, long after that practice has disappeared everywhere else in the United States. Only a few short years ago the Mustang Lounge still had occasional serve-yourself hours for its bar patrons. When the Orpheum downtown was showing first run movies in the 1960s, patrons regularly brought their own liquid refreshments, with bottles and cans rolling down the theatre's descending floor in a steady clatter.

And there is still even a Mackinac accent to those who listen closely. Thus, rather than Mack-i-naw its "Mackna City," "Mackna County," or "Mackna Island." Saint Ignace, the town, becomes "S'nignuss," and one's daughter doesn't walk her dog, but rather one's "dotter" walks her "dahg."

One constant through the years is a community pride and a palpable appreciation of living in a place of historic significance and scenic grandeur made more rich and varied by the special and unique characteristics of its people.

Henry Andress, "Chief Eagle Eye," a full-blooded Odawa, was a familiar figure on the Island through the 1960s. He squatted for years on property near Wawashkamo Golf Course and built on it a rustic log structure that served as his home even in the harshest of winters. He is pictured above in the company of his friend, Skeezix LaPine.

Flashing the victory sign with Handsome Harry Foster on Shepler's Mackinaw City dock, early 1970s.

Handsome Harry's Pardners' Club

One of the more eccentric carriage tour drivers in the late 1960s and early 1970s was middle-aged, sandy-haired, toothless, bespectacled Harry Foster who, when out of uniform, was partial to wearing a red beret.

Harry was easy-going, mild-mannered, and somehow became a favorite of the Island's summer workers. They called him "Handsome Harry." His signature greeting to one and all, "Hi, ya, Pardner," soon became the greeting du jour of the "in crowd."

Sensing a good thing, Harry printed up hundreds of cards featuring the name "Handsome Harry's Pardners' Club," entitling the bearer, for a sum certain, to the rights and privileges of membership which consisted mainly of participation in a season-ending beach party beer bash. Soon everyone, from student workers, to locals, to cottagers, wanted to be a member of Harry's not-so-exclusive fraternity. The first annual party was a roaring success. Same thing the next year. By the third year Harry was raking in so much membership money in advance of his greatly anticipated beach gala that he decided it was time to entrust the funds to one of the locals serving that summer on the Island police force. The next morning, both cop and money were gone. Gone, too, were the dreams of a modest man to be "someone," if for just one shining summer night. Gone, too, the excited anticipation of hundreds of student workers who had paid their hard-earned money expecting an evening of Island fun.

The cop wasn't seen again . . . until about 15 years later, long after a crest-fallen Harry had left Mackinac for good. Everyone in town had either forgotten the incident or themselves moved on, but I had done neither. Safe now, thanks to the expiration of the statute of limitations, the bad cop perpetrator was back on the Island and strolling the town as if nothing had happened those many years ago. I could only hope his conscience was killing him. Harry, as for you, I hope you're resting in peace, Pardner.

Speak No Evil

A local peril of which I was warned early was that of speaking ill of one Island person to another Island person. In all small towns there are close intertwinings of blood and marriage. But on Mackinac, fortified by insular living and long isolated winters, family interrelationships take on gargantuan—and often exceedingly complex—proportions. In short, you can never be sure of who is related to whom, and you can bet that an ill word about "A" will cause a reaction in "B" who, it turns out, is "A"'s half-brother, sister-in-law, or uncle by marriage. Many Islanders, in fact, are related through two or three different familial directions. As one of my Island friends told me, only partially in jest, "I'm my own Grandpaw and my own first cousin twice removed." Fifty four years after my arrival on Mackinac I am still discovering family relationships that I never knew existed.

This is not to say that Islanders never speak ill of each other. I was also told early on that the Irish are famous for carrying grudges through multiple generations. Mackinac Islanders, with their Irish influence, long periods of isolation, and generations of families living in the same small town, are no exception. My first summer on the Island, therefore, I was not surprised to hear the following, directed from one Islander to another:

"You're a son of a bitch."

After reflecting on that for a few seconds, the speaker added, "And your father was a son of a bitch."

And after another reflective pause, "And *his* father was a son of a bitch."

But the ultimate Mackinac insult is to be branded an "outsider," a "newcomer." It is a status that one doesn't easily shake. Generations of families can live on the Island without acquiring the status of an "Islander" in the eyes of other locals. I recall one incident from the summer of 1963 during the filming of NBC's *Today Show*. Two ladies, each from prominent long-time Island families, had gotten dressed up and headed off for the (old) Village Inn to celebrate over a cocktail or two the impending filming and attendant excitement. The one woman's family had come to Mackinac from Ireland during the Great Potato Famine of the 1840s. The other woman's ancestors had come as part of a soldier's family to Fort Mackinac in the late 1870s. The two, tippling on into the evening, commenced to verbally peck at one another. Soon matters escalated into a full-scale argument and insults began to fly. Other bar patrons, including me, cocked an ear toward the two, the better to hear the increasingly heated exchange. Finally, the Irish descendant turned straight on the soldier's descendent and snarled, "You . . . you . . . you're nothing but a newcomer!" Slamming down her drink, she stomped out of the bar, having delivered the ultimate Island insult and discussion-ending coup de grace.

From experience they know enough to speak no evil. This cross-section of the community enjoys a beer (or two) after a pick-up softball game in the summer of 1969. Back row L-R: lawyer-legislator Dennis Cawthorne, Murdick's Fudge owner Bob Benser, Islander Bob St. Onge, gift store owner Ron Dufina, Mustang owner Dennis Brodeur, unknown, businessman Frank Nephew, Islander Snapper Bazinaw, developer George Staffan, Islander Bob Andress. Middle row L-R: hotel clerk Mike McKillop, fudge maker Larry Senn, bartender Mike Emmons. Front row L-R: Gigi Benser, unknown, Terri Chambers, bar owner Jack Chambers, Mary Dufina.

What's in a Name ... or a Number?

One of the most endearing features of the Island, until very recently, was its street signs and street numbers or, more precisely, its lack thereof. Mackinac Island was perhaps the last city in the Western Hemisphere to have absolutely no street name signs placed at its intersections or anywhere else for that matter. Though the City has dozens of named streets, avenues, roads, and trails, not until 1986 (outside of the State Park) were any marked by an identifying sign. Even now, the ice having been broken, only a very limited number of downtown streets are demarcated.

Equally intriguing is the story of house numbers. Until 2003 no official house numbers existed. Your house number, if you opted to have one at all, was simply what you said it was. Therefore, 926 East Bluff Road, for example, might be next to no number at all which might be next to 5 East Bluff Road. We designated our house as One Lake Shore Boulevard, and why not, since who could argue otherwise. To the postman, none of this made one bit of difference since he (or she) didn't deliver anyway, all Island mail being received only though post offices boxes located in the post office building located at no number (or was it 176 or 593?) Market Street.

All of this ended, or should have, when the City hired an out-of-state firm to assign numbers to every structure on the Island using a geo-positioning system. Somehow, compared to the old days, it all seemed rather mechanical and unromantic. Life at what is now 3439 Lakeshore Boulevard (formerly One Lake Shore Boulevard) goes on, however, as before.

Still, it is not quite that simple. It turns out that on Mackinac, street names tend to be fluid and shifting. Old maps say the main street of the Island is named Water Street. Later maps identify it as Huron Street. The geo-positioning company fixed it, prosaically, as Main Street. Hoban Street runs in front of the Village Inn downtown but slightly older maps say Hoban Avenue runs through the middle of Harrisonville while current maps say the same road is Cadotte Avenue. Our home, on the northwest side of the Island, we always said (and every map confirms) is located on Lake Shore Boulevard. Newer city maps (again prepared by outside professionals) said it is located on State Highway M-185. Only when I threatened to stop paying utility bills from the Department of Public Works and the electric company that listed our property as being on M-185 did I get them to change it back to the rightful Lake Shore Boulevard. I urged my British Landing neighbors to do likewise. What red-blooded American, I ask you, wouldn't prefer living at One Lake Shore Boulevard rather than the bureaucratic, humdrum address of 3439 State Highway M-185?

As recently as January 2013, the *Lansing State Journal* reported that Grand Hotel was located at 286 Grand Avenue (undoubtedly because that's what the Grand itself said was its address). Trouble is, the only Grand Avenue on city maps is located about a mile northwest of the Grand and the new building numbers have four digits, not three, and none begin with "2".

Over the years, there have also been fun and games with Island phone numbers. In the local phone book for years Mrs. Chester Keogh of the East Bluff listed her dog Frederick's name and number, perhaps a first in canine history anywhere.

The Detroit News

AIRPLANE EDITION

FRIDAY, JULY 29, 1960, VOL. 87, NO. 342 — THE HOME NEWSPAPER—ESTABLISHED 1873 — 4 SECTIONS—52 PAGES — 10¢

MURDER ON MACKINAC!
WIDOW'S BODY FOUND

Nixon Promises Hard Campaign in All 50 States

(Related Stories and Pictures on Pages 10A, 14B, 6C and 7C)

By ELIE ABEL
Chief of Our Washington Bureau

CHICAGO, July 29. — Richard M. Nixon started running scared today in what promises to be the longest, most strenuous presidential campaign the country ever has seen. He said he would campaign in every state.

A few hours after accepting the GOP nomination, Nixon went to work framing battle plans and policies. His answer to the "new frontier" promised by Senator Kennedy, of Massachusetts, the Democratic standard-bearer, was a "better America" that "will not tolerate being pushed around by anybody, any place."

Discarded streamers and confetti were still being swept from Chicago's pavements when Nixon held his first strategy meeting with the Republican National Committee.

HAWAII FIRST

He planned to spend the week end in Chicago conferring with his running mate, United Na-

Kickback Defendant Faces Court

'I DON'T WANT TO BE LOCKED UP ANY MORE'
—AP Wirephoto
Nurse Frances Newman Comforts Gordon Dickerson

Suit Filed Against Chrysler

Stockholder Asks Firm Collect for Newberg Deals

By RALPH R. WATTS
Detroit News Automotive Writer

A Chrysler Corp. stockholder has filed suit against the company to recover any damages suffered by the firm because of interests which ex-President William C. Newberg formerly held in suppliers.

The action followed disclosure yesterday by L. L. Colbert, company chairman and president, of the names of two firms in which Newberg held interests.

The stockholder's suit was brought by Robert Markewich, a New York attorney who owns about 100 Chrysler shares.

"We consider the damages caused the corporation to be

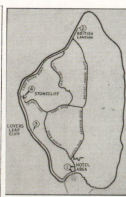

Slaying Motive Is Mystery

Woman Clothed but Shoeless in Island Woods

By BOYD SIMMONS
Of The Detroit News Staff

MACKINAC ISLAND, July 29.—The body of a 49-year-old Dearborn widow, who vanished on a walk last Sunday, was found last night in a thickly wooded area near the southwest shore of this historic straits island.

Mrs. Frances Lacey, 80½ Lafayette south, apparently was murdered after she left the Murray Hotel and headed for British Landing, about 3½ miles away, to meet relatives at a summer cottage.

Details of the tragedy were scarce as State Police troopers stood guard at the scene and awaited an examination of the

Murder

On July 24, 1960, just 32 days after I arrived on the Island, against almost impossible odds there was committed in broad daylight on Mackinac Island the perfect crime. Frances Lacey, a 49-year-old Dearborn (Michigan) widow was murdered, strangled with her own underwear, on a hot Sunday morning during the Chicago to Mackinac yacht races, on a road over which that day thousands of persons would pass on bike or on foot.

Incredibly, no one saw it happen, nor did anyone witness the perpetrator drag the victim from Lake Shore Boulevard and conceal the corpse under a pile of brush just beyond a stone-pillared gate that lay in front of a path leading up a hill to the sprawling Stonecliffe mansion.

The entire saga, were it made into a movie, I think would eclipse *Somewhere in Time* at the box office. The story has almost every element of high drama: baying bloodhounds in pursuit along a darkened rain-slicked boardwalk, an all-night open air vigil alongside the corpse, policemen and plain clothes detectives on bicycles, family relatives as initial suspects, carriage drivers questioned in dingy backrooms, and an old carefully guarded mansion occupied by people with English accents. All of this set against a backdrop of crashing waves on a pebble-strewn beach, horses and buggies, an old fort, places with names like Devil's Kitchen and Lover's Leap and townspeople buzzing with the latest gossip, suspicions, and rumors. In the words of the July 31, 1960 edition of the *Detroit News,* "Had a novelist (written) this, it would have been branded far-fetched."

Mrs. Lacey had come to the Island a day before she disappeared. She had accompanied her daughter and son-in-law who had rented a small cottage a short distance from Michael Early's refreshment stand at British Landing. Mrs. Lacey, however, had checked into the Murray Hotel downtown and told her daughter she would walk the three and a half miles to British Landing and meet her the next morning at 11 a.m. She never arrived. Alarmed, her family contacted the Mackinac Island police, and by Monday morning a massive search for her was underway.

I clearly remember that the immediate assumption on the street was that she had met with foul play, odd in retrospect given the fact that serious crime (in those days) was a rarity on the Island. That night I was walking back to my housing on Market Street when Bob Roe, driving night taxi, pulled up and asked me to ride with him and his party of two on a run to British Landing. I demurred, but Bob was insistent. I hopped aboard, paying little attention to the couple in the back of the cab. When at last we had clip-clopped our long, dark way to British Landing and discharged our two passengers, Bob turned the cab around and breathed a sigh of relief. His passengers, he said, had been the daughter and son-in-law of the missing Mrs. Lacey. On our way back to town on the shore road we passed unknowingly within 50 feet from where Frances Lacey's body would be found.

Over the next four days, the Island was scoured by state police troopers, the tiny local police force, Mackinac county sheriff's deputies, Coast Guardsmen, volunteers, and even Boy Scout Troop 66 of Detroit. Bloodhounds were called in and picked up a trail twice, only to be foiled by a light rain. It was later discovered that the bloodhounds at one point led searchers within yards of where the body was later found, only to be called off because their handlers thought the hounds had lost the scent.

Meanwhile, back in Detroit, a couple just returned from a weekend trip to the Island, walked into the Redford post of the state police and reported that while riding a tandem bike

on the shore road the previous Sunday they had found a purse on the pavement with Mrs. Lacey's identification inside. Acting on details supplied by the couple, State Police zeroed in on the spot where Stonecliffe's gate intersects with Lake Shore Boulevard. At 7:18 p.m. Thursday, July 28, they found the body not far from the road's edge on an incline covered with fallen pine boughs.

State Police later theorized that Mrs. Lacey had sat down to rest, perhaps on a log near the side of the road, and taken off her low-heeled walking shoes. When her assailant approached, she tried to fight him off by hitting him with a pair of high-heeled shoes she was carrying in a plastic bag. Police theorized he grabbed the bag from her, struck and choked her and then dragged her unconscious inside the Stonecliffe gate. There he threw the bag containing the shoes under a rotting boat, assaulted her, and carried her further up the incline.

When found, Mrs. Lacey was lying face down with her head pointed to the lakeshore. Her underwear was wrapped around her neck, her blouse pulled up to her shoulders and her skirt to her hips. Her glasses were near her left hand, her jacket missing. With twilight setting in, state police roped off the site and, to preserve all clues, two troopers kept a night-long vigil over the body.

An autopsy later that morning established the cause of death as strangulation and the instrument her underwear. On Lake Shore Boulevard police found Mrs. Lacey's dental plate ground into the roadway by passing carriages. Seventeen days later, her wallet, taken from her purse, was found empty in a row of hedges below Grand Hotel. Her gold watch, stripped from her wrist, was never recovered.

The search for the killer immediately launched into high gear. One Island worker was detained by police even before a body was found, then detained again afterward. Employees who left the Island between Sunday and Thursday were tracked down across the country and grilled. Carriage drivers were questioned. A former mental patient and an Islander just released from federal prison were scrutinized. Tourists and locals were not ruled out, nor was Mrs. Lacey's family. Police and a newspaper reporter paid a visit to the Stonecliffe mansion, then owned and utilized by Moral Re-Armament. There they received a decidedly cool reception. "We prefer not to speak to anyone. We prefer not to enter the matter at all. Good day," was the curt response. And with that the door was firmly shut.

By the time the active investigation ended, over 22 state police officers had worked on the case and nearly 400 persons were questioned. State police eventually concluded that the cycling couple who found Mrs. Lacey's purse had just missed seeing the perpetrator, and perhaps the body. In all probability, he had seen them. Police continued sifting through tips

Detectives and reporters stand near the Stonecliffe gates on Lakeshore Boulevard while state police troopers can be seen beyond and near where Mrs. Lacey's body was found.

and clues, and for a number of years afterward staked out the murder site on the anniversary date, hoping that just maybe the killer might return.

Perhaps a dozen years later, in the early 1970s, a retired state police trooper who had been one of the chief investigators on the case told Jack Chambers and me that his own theory was that the killer was someone staying at Stonecliffe and that, discovering what their guest had done and fearing a public relations disaster, MRA personnel stalled investigators long enough to hustle the now unwelcome guest off the Island and perhaps out of the country.

There are good reasons to think the theory has some validity. A University of Michigan student told State Police that two weeks before the murder he encountered a nude man sitting on a log with his back to the road at almost the exact same spot from which Mrs. Lacey was abducted. "The man spoke with a distinct English accent," the student recounted, lending credence to the Stonecliffe connection.

On the other hand it strains credulity to think an MRA guest would be the kind to also engage in petty thievery of the kind committed by Mrs. Lacey's killer. The fact that her wallet was found long afterward near Grand Hotel, far from Stonecliffe, also seems to counter any theory that the murderer sought refuge at the mansion, was shielded behind closed doors, and then quickly spirited off the Island.

Fifty two years later, in 2012, I walked and poked around the Lacey crime scene. I was struck again by how nearly impossible it would have been to carry out undetected murder by strangulation in broad daylight on a Sunday morning in July on a very busy Lake Shore Boulevard. I wondered if the owners of the two new homes constructed on either side of the spot where Mrs. Lacey was found even knew of the gruesome crime committed long ago just steps from their front doors.

Who did it? It remains Mackinac's greatest mystery.

Jack Chambers (left) listens to Bill Doyle regale Gov. William Milliken (right) at the grand opening of the new Village Inn, June 1981.

Three to Remember

My early days on the Island were marked by an acquaintance with three colorful and often controversial figures. Each, quite apart from one another, would play prominent roles in many Mackinac events of the 1960s, '70s, and '80s.

Jack Chambers, Bill Doyle, and Harry Ryba were unforgettable people by any measure. Certainly there were others, less flamboyant, whose contributions to the Island were arguably more profound, valuable, and long lasting. Many of those people are described in the pages that follow. Still, the story of each one of these three provides a window into the Mackinac Island of that era.

Bill Doyle

I was introduced to Wilfird Francis Xavier Doyle (1897-1988) my first summer on the Island, fittingly, by Jack Chambers. Jack thought Doyle and I could perhaps be a good "tag team" because Doyle was a prominent 60-ish Lansing lobbyist who specialized in entertaining politicians visiting the Island and I was a 20-year-old political wannabe with a prodigious memory for politicians' names and faces.

Doyle had been elected as a Republican to the State Senate for a single term in 1932 from an Upper Peninsula district which included Mackinac Island. Doyle stayed on in Lansing first in a minor appointive position under Republican Governor Frank D. Fitzgerald, then as a lobbyist for an association representing chain retail stores such as Kroger and J.C. Penney. By the time he retired in 1964 he was the most highly compensated—and most powerful—lobbyist in the state capitol.

During the late 1930s he signed a contract to help promote and publicize the Island, then acquired one of the magnificent East Bluff homes that, in the wake of the Great Depression could be bought for practically nothing. In 1939 Governor Luren Dickinson appointed Doyle to the Mackinac State Park Commission where he remained a member—with two notable interruptions—for the next 45 years.

Shrewd, engaging, possessed of a sly Irish wit, a gifted storyteller prone to some exaggeration, Doyle immersed himself in all things Mackinac. Never one to shun the limelight, Doyle became known across the state, with an assist from himself, as the "King of Mackinac." When in 1941 he sensed he might lose his Commission seat with the coming of new Democratic Governor Murray D. Van Wagoner, he quietly convinced the Legislature to add a seat to the then five-member body to be reserved for a "resident commissioner" owning property on the Island and to be nominated by the Island's mayor, for which vacancy Doyle would be the only obvious choice. The resident commissioner gambit temporarily back-fired on Doyle in 1947. Feuding with Grand Hotel owner W. Stewart Woodfill, Doyle failed to get the new mayor's (Alan Sawyer) nomination for reappointment by the Governor, and was side-lined until Republican Governor Kim Sigler appointed him to a different vacancy on the Commission later in the year.[1]

In 1949, now serving as Commission chair, Doyle ruled that the new Democratic Governor, G. Mennen Williams, sitting on the Commission ex-officio, did not have the right to cast a tie-breaking vote to elect his own hand-picked Democratic choice for chairman. Having so ruled, Doyle declared that since the Governor's vote didn't count, a tie vote existed and that therefore the incumbent chair, himself, would carry on for another term. In 1951, at the next election for chairman, the Governor was again blocked from voting. A 3-3 partisan tie vote for Chair resulted and Doyle ruled himself chairman still again since no one had a majority to replace him. Doyle's parliamentary rulings were technically correct but politically outrageous.

Williams had his revenge. He refused to re-appoint Doyle when his term as Commissioner expired in 1955, and Doyle was again side-lined. Only when Democrat John Swainson was elected Governor, and after the foxy Doyle has ingratiated himself to the new chief executive by working to secure an official taxpayer-paid Lansing residence for the Governor, did Doyle in 1961 regain a seat on the Commission. He didn't relinquish it (being re-appointed by Governors Romney and Milliken) until, with encouragement from the Democratic Blanchard Administration, he stepped aside in 1984 at age 86 on Doyle's condition that a retirement party be thrown in his honor at the Governor's residence.

During my early years on Mackinac, Doyle was protective of Mackinac Island Carriage Tours, Inc. and fancied himself the benefactor of local interests and the local government, sometimes to the detriment of his own State Park Commission. He enjoyed stoking political fights, often over trivial matters, with his fellow Irish (but Democratic)

---

[1] The state law was subsequently changed, probably again the work of Doyle, dropping the requirement that the Governor appoint as resident commissioner a person nominated by the Mayor of Mackinac Island.

long-time Commissioners Walter Murray and James Dunnigan. Sometimes he seemed to create or invent problems so that he could take the lead in solving them. He was fond of suggesting the need for Attorney General opinions when he was on the losing side of a Commission vote, often playing the lawyer he was not. Doyle also savored the perks then available to Commissioners, including state-owned carriages with state-paid drivers on call, and the accompanying social and political prestige of office. Still, his devotion to and love of the Island was beyond any doubt.

Jack Chambers

John T. Chambers (1926-2005), my boss at Carriage Tours, was intelligent, witty, acerbic, controversial, and outspoken. He was frequently sought out by visiting big-city news reporters and could be counted on for a memorable quote. Born in Chicago in 1926, and plagued by bad eyesight as a youth, he came from a long line of early Irish settlers of the Island. When his mother died at a young age, Jack came to Mackinac to live with his spinster aunt and bachelor uncle. His grandfather, "Cannonball Bill" Chambers, operated a restaurant at British Landing on the Island's northwest side. Young Chambers joined the U.S. Merchant Marines during World War II and came back to the Island in 1947 to operate his horse-drawn milk route and drive his horse-drawn taxi for hire.

Ever the maverick, Jack managed to evade the forced consolidation of horse-drawn tour and taxi operations in 1948, but exasperated stockholders of the new consolidated company eventually made it worth his while to throw in with them. He quickly rose to become assistant manager of operations which is where I encountered him when I first came to the Island to work for his employer, Mackinac Island Carriage Tours Inc.

In the mid-1960's he left MICT and bought with Dennis Brodeur the Village Inn on Main Street, expanded it, and worked as restaurateur-saloon keeper for the next 15 years. He dubbed his modest private residence "Manure Manor," and at various times he served as the City building inspector (an unpaid position for which he had no formal training), as the elected City supervisor (the only duties of which were to sit on the three member tax assessment board of appeals), and valuable member of the Board of Public Works.

For the first 35 years of his life, Jack Chambers did not drink. For the next 35 years (and more), after the first of three divorces, he more than made up for lost time. By the 1970s and 1980s, by actual count of Island bartenders (it would become a sport for them), he would on many days consume 30 to 35 beers. At one point, probably in the mid-1980s, I calculated that he had personally consumed at least 150,000 beers. By the time of his passing in 2005, I'm sure his life-time total consumption has risen to well over 200,000, the equivalent of at least 1,200 barrels of beer.

Through it all, Jack was a special friend to me and to many young Islanders and Island employees. He treated us generously, made us laugh, shared his wisdom, and generally looked out for us. It was he who single-handedly convinced the Chamber of Commerce to hire the young 22-year-old to be its manager in 1962. He invited me to be his guest at his

Sharing a laugh and a beer with Jack Chambers, 1981.

winter home in Fort Lauderdale, Florida for Spring Break in 1965 when I badly needed a change of scenery away from the rigors of Harvard Law. He convinced me to make my first-ever winter visit to the Island in late January 1966 when his friends threw him a very liquid "Life Begins at Forty" birthday party. When I was elected to the Legislature later in 1966, no one was more proud. In 1978 he sold me the back lot of his downtown property which three years later became the site of the new Village Inn on Hoban Street. At the bar, he was our best customer, and though increasingly given to politically incorrect verbal observations, with his storytelling and commentary he was the center of all attention.

Harry Ryba

Harry Ryba (1907-1996), with an elfish 5-foot-5 exterior and puckish grin, was restless, driven, and self-made. "The Fudge King of Mackinac," as he was dubbed by the PR man he hired, came to Mackinac in 1959 one year before my arrival, and I became acquainted with him, too, that first summer.

Ryba was born in Detroit and after World War II opened there a candy store where he made a product billed as "Mackinac Island Fudge" and traveled to fairs and trade shows marketing it. Fudge, of course, had been Mackinac's most famous product since 1889 when Newton Jerome ("Rome") Murdick opened his store. His son Gould succeeded to the business but sold it to his chief candy cook Harold May around the time of World War II. In the ensuing years and during my time, there was both a May's (the "oldest" fudge store), a Murdick's (opened by one of Gould's relatives in 1947 and promptly billed as the "original" fudge store), as well as Selma's, Joanne's, Suzan's, Kilwin's, Murray's, and Sanders'. By the 1990s Island stores were collectively selling nearly a half million pounds of fudge annually.

It was Harry Ryba, however, who revolutionized the Island fudge scene. He moved fudge-making to his shop's front window to attract gawking passers-by, blew the sweet smell of fresh candy out his front door, offered ten flavors, put his product in pink boxes and pink shopping bags, and advertised on radio and billboards.

To the rest of the fudge-making community, which marketed their products as if it were still 1889, Harry and his Ryba Fudge was an unwelcome intrusion. Harry's personality and rapid-fire chatter did not always help. One generally laudatory 1979 profile in the *Detroit Free Press* Sunday magazine described him as "loved by some and testily unloved by others . . .with the soul of a carnival pitchman and the heart of a hustler . . . (he has) an ability to rub people wrong . . . (he) rarely minces words . . . a diplomat he is not."

But Harry was also on to something bigger. The man who had never before done business on Mackinac despite producing and selling his Mackinac candy, saw something few others on Mackinac saw. "If a guy had come here in 1945 or 1946," he told the *Detroit Free Press,* "he could have picked up the whole town for $60,000." When the Mackinac Bridge and I-75 opened in the late 1950s, "I knew that was it . . . all those people coming up North. If I'd had any money then I would have bought all kinds of property. But I didn't so I just leased one shop."

Soon he did have the money, however, and "whatever was for sale (on Mackinac) I bought. I grabbed it. When I got here, these (local) people weren't business people. They had no vision. They didn't see the potential."

But Harry saw the potential. His one fudge store soon expanded to multiple Island locations. He struck a deal with the State Park Commission, before my time on it, to lease and renovate the thoroughly run-down Island House hotel, later bought and renovated the Lake View Hotel, acquired 395 rental bike licenses ("licenses to steal," according to an old Island saying), opened a pancake shop in one location and a bar-restaurant in another, and constructed a mini-mall opposite the Lake View with a laundromat, grocery, game room, and assorted other offerings.

It was Harry who coined the name "fudgie" for tourist day-trippers coming to the Island for a quick tour and leaving with a box of confections tucked under their arms. In time, the name "fudgie" would be synonymous with a tourist coming to any place in northern Michigan.

Twenty years after he first came to Mackinac, the *Free Press* said, "Harry is still considered (by some) a brash outsider (who doesn't) have a proper respect for the Island's historical integrity."

Others saw a softer side. "If a man ever needed help, the first man that would be there is Harry Ryba," said Jack Chambers who one newspaper dubbed as Harry's "affectionate adversary." His son-in-law, daughter, and grandchildren carried on many of his enterprises after his death.

Harry Ryba serving up his speciality.

MRA
MORAL RE-ARMAMENT

MRA THEATER

MACKINAC ISLAND
MICHIGAN

On the Island of Mackinac stand the Moral Re-Armament Assembly Buildings, where year by year people of every nation, race and color come from every continent, for training in an idea to unite men and remake the world.

IT IS NOT WHO IS RIGHT, BUT WHAT IS RIGHT

Moral Re-Armament

In my early days on the Island, the "elephant in the room" was an organization called Moral Re-Armament. By the time I first arrived on Mackinac, Moral Re-Armament had already been ensconced on the Island for two decades. From its scraggly beginnings in 1942 in one dilapidated hotel, MRA's Mackinac presence had by 1960 ballooned to the point where it seemed to consume much of the twenty percent of the land area of the Island that was not state park. Stonecliffe, Silver Birches, Chateau Beaumont, La Chance, Bonnie Doon, Pine Cottage, Maple View, Mission House, and numerous smaller houses in the Mission area were all MRA-owned. Rumors were that MRA was out to acquire Grand Hotel. All of this in addition to the wide swath of Mission (sometimes called Cedar) Point where just a half dozen years earlier there was only vacant, semi-swampy land, and which now held a great conference hall, theatre, sound stage, and dormitories housing hundreds of people.

Onto the sleepiest, most provincial and insular of American small towns, MRA had super-imposed almost overnight an international presence that brought to Mackinac's shores world leaders, surrogates of world leaders, and thousands of idealistic adherents from all over the globe. Buddhist monks in saffron robes, Indian chiefs in full headdress, African tribal princes in flowing garments, and Scotsmen in kilts crowded Mackinac's streets and docks on a daily basis.

The result was local culture shock and, by the time of my arrival, resentment, suspicion, and division of epic proportions. To many locals, eventual total takeover of the Island by MRA, economically and politically, seemed not at all improbable. One MRA executive sat on the City Council. The Island doctor, Joe Solomon was an MRA-er and by 1963 he was also the mayor. MRA banned alcohol, smoking, cosmetics, and even double beds on its own property. What might be in store for the rest of the Island?

Dr. Frank Buchman, MRA's founder, sits at the center surrounded by adherents in front of its temporary world headquarters, the Island House in late summer 1945.

Originally known as the Oxford Group, Moral Re-Armament's founder was Dr. Frank Buchman, a Pennsylvania-born Lutheran minister who in 1915 accompanied an evangelist on a religious tour of the Far East and India. Organizing services which sometimes attracted 60,000 people at a time, Buchman gained valuable experience for later travels of his own on which he was accompanied by young followers dedicated to his belief that changing the moral and spiritual lives of a few leading men could result in change sweeping an entire nation. Buchman and his adherents preached "The Four Absolutes," absolute honesty, purity, unselfishness, and love, directed by God's "guidance" and involving self-evaluation and open confession of one's shortcomings at small "house parties." Oxford University in England became a leading source of youthful Buchman recruits, soon providing an identifying name for the movement. When World War II broke out, Buchman began speaking out for "moral re-armament" of individuals and nations and the group's focus shifted from strictly spiritual concerns to encompass issues of political ideology. His movement bore a new name, "Moral Re-Armament," and Buchman now targeted world leaders to be won over and through them, the masses. Emphasis was now placed on changing entire nations, small gatherings giving way to mass meetings, house parties to world assemblies.[1]

What MRA lacked was a place to call its own, a place to host world leaders, train individuals in MRA methods for changing the world and produce the movies and plays that would carry the MRA message. Just prior to U.S. entry into World War II, MRA produced and took on the road a play called *You Can Defend America,* which portrayed American labor and management working in a common cause. Mr. and Mrs. Henry Ford hosted Buchman during the play's showing in Detroit. Hearing that Buchman was looking for a home for his "factory of ideas," and perhaps thinking of Mackinac's Depression – induced excess of hotel rooms, Mrs. Ford suggested the Island. She soon enlisted Michigan Governor Murray D. Van Wagoner and MISPC Chairman Wilfird F. Doyle in the cause and in the spring of 1942 the State of Michigan leased to MRA the Island House Hotel which it had recently acquired for delinquent back taxes.

MRA volunteers from around the world were soon at work refurbishing the thoroughly decrepit edifice. The place was "in terrible shape . . . hardly describable, filth and ice on the floor, grease all over the kitchen . . . it was just a mess," MRA volunteers recalled. By July 9, 1942, the transformed hotel was opened as MRA's first permanent facility. Soon visitors from all over the world began arriving on an Island starved for tourists first by the Depression and then war. "Without MRA," remembers one person, "you could have shot a cannon down the main street of Mackinac and never hit anyone."

---

1   Buchman had his share of critics, especially Tom Driberg, a member of the British House of Commons.

THE WORD

- MRA Tax Squeeze -

The MRA, professing "Absolute Honesty", paid taxes on Mackinac Island for more than fifteen years. Two years ago they claimed tax exemption. Why, after honestly paying taxes for fifteen years, did MRA file for exemption?

It seems that the MRA never intended to pay taxes on Mackinac Island. Two questions keep coming to our mind:

<u>Could the MRA have obtained tax exemption in their first few years of occupation here?</u> The answer to this is a simple "no". Why? Because everybody would have been wise to the move, losing them the local support.

<u>Why did MRA file for exemption two years ago saying for fifteen years that they would pay taxes?</u> The answer is that after being soft-soaped into trusting MRA for fifteen years we, the people, are no longer in a position to oppose a group so firmly established here. They have enough votes of their own members and local supporters to do as they please. MRA can now use economic and social pressures against any opposition. These same pressures would have been most unpopular ten years ago.

MRA methods for gaining tax exemption have been:

1) An outward claim that they will always be glad to pay taxes, to-wit: two letters on file with the City Council;

2) Maneuvering their people and their puppets into positions of local government so that at their convenience and beckoning, tax exemption could be lain at their feet;

3) Using laws meant for legitimate, non-profit religious and benevolent organizations, they have qualified their so called "non-profit" institution for tax exemption;

4) Using the veiled threat that if government officals don't cooperate in helping MRA obtain tax exemption, the MRA will not then be willing to make a "gift" of $20,000 in lieu of taxes. In other words, if local officials opposed tax exemption but MRA obtained it anyway, the city would be left with nothing. Go along with MRA, on the other hand, and we at least have a small drop in the bucket. (Maybe this is coercion.)

The Word, financed by Jack Chambers and written by college student Charlie Moore, appeared in the early 1960s as a local voice of opposition to MRA's local presence. MRA leaders were not amused.

With the end of the war, MRA embarked on building projects that gave local Islanders for the first time ever year-round employment. By 1947, MRA had outgrown the Island House and began buying up individual properties in great numbers. In 1957 an 800-seat theatre became the first new building constructed by MRA. Construction of the magnificent Great Hall, employing one hundred locals and 45 MRA volunteers, occurred in 1955-56. Dormitories were built in 1956-57 and in 1959 the largest movie soundstage outside of Hollywood.

But the bloom began to come off MRA's Mackinac rose in the early 1960s. Upon completion of most of MRA's big building projects, local labor crews were laid off. Islanders muttered about MRA's intense evangelizing, strict Puritanism, and creeping intrusion into local politics. MRA's sometimes cavalier approach to the Island's auto ban and its claim of tax exemption for its extensive properties didn't help. MRA even maintained its own fire truck and volunteer firemen, some said, for fear the local department might not choose to rush to an MRA fire. It was also said, and believed by many, that MRA built its tall glass observation tower near the Great Hall for the express purpose of looking down on the town and spying on its local enemies.

I was told by City Clerk Lenore Goodheart that MRA had "placed a tail" on me, although why the Harvard Law School student-Chamber of Commerce manager should rate such a distinction I was not sure unless it was my friendship with Jack Chambers, arch-enemy of MRA.

Bill Doyle had long ago shifted from welcoming friend to outspoken foe, motivated in part perhaps by the realization that MRA's growing Island influence made the "King of the Island" potentially less relevant. Stewart Woodfill and Otto Lang also now kept their distance.

In the summer of 1963 long-simmering antagonisms reached a fever pitch. There appeared in all local mailboxes each week an unsigned publication named *The Word*. In fact, *The Word* was conceived and financed by the ubiquitous Jack Chambers and written by Charlie Moore, a recent Albion College graduate who worked for Carriage Tours, of which Jack was assistant manager. Its effect on the locals was to crystallize their growing resentment of MRA. Although he never publically acknowledged his connection to *The Word*, the quotable Chambers later told the *Detroit Free Press*, referring to MRA, "I'm a burr in their saddle and a thorn in their side."

As a friend of both Jack and Charlie, I was one of the very few people who knew for certain the persons responsible for *The Word*. Though I had nothing to do with its publication and stayed clear of its fallout, I was sworn to secrecy, a commitment which, after 50 years, I suppose I am free to abrogate.

The Peter Howard Library, named for Frank Buchman's successor, was built on shorefront to serve students of the new Mackinac College, successor to MRA. Widely criticized for its modern design, out of character for the Island, it was mercifully torn down by a later owner of the property, John Shufelt of Mission Point Resort.

In the fall of 1965 the matter boiled over. In late October the United Press, the national wire service used by hundreds of U. S. newspaper and radio and television stations, quoted MRA executive Basil Entwistle as saying, "Of course you know there are Communists on this Island. They're not foolish in Moscow. They've placed Communists here. Since you've been talking to people in the village, you've undoubtedly been talking to Communists." The wire service story added, "MRA spokesmen speak darkly of "the saloon and brothel owners of Mackinac."

Bill Doyle sprang into action. Supported by Commissioner Jim Dunnigan, he introduced a Commission resolution that made the front page of the October 30 *Detroit News*. Under the heading "Mackinac Isle Vice Tale Hit, Officials Demand Proof or MRA Apology," the *News* reported: "Mackinac Island State Park Commissioners feel their sleepy Victorian-era paradise has been vandalized by intruders . . . They don't believe the Island . . . is brimming with brothels, Communists, and saloon keepers . . .The Commission voted . . . to demand proof or a retraction of the charges."

If MRA failed to prove its charges, the resolution said, it should make a complete and public retraction together with a public apology to the people of Mackinac Island and the State of Michigan. Failing that, the resolution continued, Attorney General Frank J. Kelley should be asked to pursue libel charges.

No one on the Island doubted that MRA's "saloon keeper" (and probably "brothel keeper") reference was aimed at Jack Chambers, Village Inn proprietor and suspected—but unproven—force behind *The Word*. Enjoying the fury to which he had finally driven MRA, Chambers jokingly opined that since "all the females on the Island are giving it away" the brothel claim was "just as phony as the charge of Communists on Mackinac Island."

Not much more was ever heard of the matter, however, save for the reaction of West Bluffer Rita Bankard who told the *Muskegon Chronicle*, in a story headlined, 'She Rises to Defend Her Island,' "They're libeling the Island . . . There's something mysterious about that bunch. If MRAers are told to avoid the residents, the latter are only too happy to keep it that way."

Nineteen sixty five, the year I graduated from Harvard Law School and ended my time as manager of the Island Chamber of Commerce, proved to be a seminal year for MRA, too. Frank Buchman had died in 1961 at the age of 83 and was succeeded by Peter Howard, a former Fleet Street journalist and long-time understudy of Buchman. In contrast to Buchman, he believed that working with young people held the key to changing the world. At a 1964 Youth Conference on the Island, MRA encouraged a "Sing Out" to spread its message. There grew out of it what became known as *Up With People* which by 1967 had casts of young people spreading the MRA message through music productions all over the world. The net result, however, was the splitting of MRA into two factions with two essentially different philosophies and tactics. When Peter Howard died very unexpectedly in 1965, MRA was dealt still another blow.

Before his death, Howard, pursing his emphasis on youth, conceived the idea of converting the Mackinac properties into a college. Under the leadership of the aforementioned Entwistle, the conversion occurred. The new college, technically separate from MRA, added still more buildings including classrooms, faculty housing (now Lesley Court condominiums), and an ultra-modern lakefront library (mercifully torn down in the 1990s by subsequent property owner John Shufelt). It also acquired a top-flight faculty and a prestigious president, S. Douglas Cornell. Mackinac College opened in September 1966, attracted students from 81 countries, and closed its doors in 1970. Economic challenges and a winter-time isolation not suited to active, restless young people doomed it to failure after graduating just a single class of students. The last vestiges of MRA withdrew from the Island, the book finally closing on its momentous more than quarter century Mackinac presence.

During its years on the Island, MRA made occasional attempts at recruiting locals, but while some were sympathetic to the cause, no one – to the best of my knowledge – was ever actually converted to active participation. In addition to their affinity for the occasional stiff drink so frowned on by MRA, the largely Catholic year-round population was also discouraged from getting too close by the Church's basic antipathy to Buchman and his cause.

I did not personally know any member of MRA or its successor college during their best years on the Island, but later, long after MRA had abandoned Mackinac, I did get to know some of the handful of adherents who stayed on in the Mackinac community. I found them, to a person, to be warm, sincere, and of exceptional good character.[1]

---

1. For a well-done thesis on this subject see "Moral Re-Armament and Mackinac Island," by Catherine M. Edwards, Hillsdale College, May 1994.

One duty of a Chamber manager, at least in my case, was crowning the Lilac Queen. Receiving the 1963 tiara, above, was Nancy Pfeiffelman. At right is Queen's court member Cindy Francis.

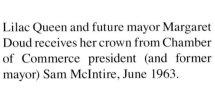

Lilac Queen and future mayor Margaret Doud receives her crown from Chamber of Commerce president (and former mayor) Sam McIntire, June 1963.

Chamber of Commerce Manager

In late Spring 1962, after a one year hiatus, I decided I would have at age 22 just one last Mackinac Island summer fling before embarking on the really serious business of a legal education at Harvard Law. I would return to work one last time for Carriage Tours and Jack Chambers. He had other plans. The Island's Chamber of Commerce manager, Barry McGuire, had taken another position, and suddenly there was a vacancy. On the very day I was packing my car to leave Albion College for the last time, baccalaureate diploma in hand, I received an urgent phone call.

"You don't want to work for Carriage Tours," the caller informed me.

"I don't?" I said in a voice crossed between apprehension and incredulity.

"No," Jack Chambers said, "You want to run our Chamber of Commerce, and I'm going to see that it happens."

So the stage was set for me to be the sole interviewee a few days later when the Chamber's Board of Directors convened at the Chippewa Hotel to see first-hand what Jack Chambers brought them. The Board was composed of the businessmen who ran the Island's commercial enterprises, the town's "establishment": the kindly Otto W. Lang, operations chief of Arnold Transit, whose initials perfectly fit both his demeanor and his appearance; Nathan Shayne, owner of the Chippewa Hotel, who seemed to man by himself 24-hours-a-day his hotel's front desk and whose Pink Pony Bar mainly catered to elderly ladies' tour groups; my patron Jack Chambers, assistant manager of Carriage Tours; Dan Musser, dapper 32-year-old surrogate and nephew of W.S. Woodfill, legendary owner of the Island's landmark Grand Hotel; Dennis Brodeur, popular young owner of the Wandrie Restaurant; Sam McIntire, a former state police body guard to the Governor and who, in a few short years of ownership, had transformed the sleepy Iroquois into a premier hotel and dining spot; Tony Trayser, gift shop owner who to many personified the "grab-it-and-run" merchants who hustled their money south at the end of each season and contributed little to the community; Bob Benjamin, photographer and camera shop owner whose Island roots

went back several generations; Hugh Rudolph, business manager of Arnold Transit, city assessor and son-in-law of the prominent Prentiss M. Brown, former U.S. Senator, banker and utility executive whose Island and Straits area property holdings were extensive; and Maria Moeller, the Board's only female, gregarious, finely-dressed and coifed, and owner of one of the Island's few quality gift shops.

By the end of the meeting, Jack Chambers' recommendation carried the day. I was hired for the munificent salary of $2,000 for the season, plus room and board. (When I left the position in September 1965 my salary had risen to the princely sum of $2,500.) The Chamber's total annual operating budget, I soon learned, was pitifully small. Mainly it funded the printing and mailing of promotional brochures and the general overhead of two mainland tourist information offices plus a headquarters, a cramped information booth on Main Street where I would work for a total of four summers. My challenge was to drum up as much free Island publicity as possible simply because there was no money for paid advertising. In between, I ran community events like the Lilac Festival, crowned queens, and chased Island merchants who conveniently "forgot" to pay their annual Chamber dues. Some cagily paid up just before a new printing of promotional brochures which included the names of Chamber members, then skipped the intervening years before a new printing.

I worked with civic and business leaders from the Straits area, wrote press releases, entertained visiting travel writers, testified before state legislative committees, and generally did whatever I could do to promote Island commerce and tourism. This I did while my Harvard Law School classmates were clerking at prestigious Wall Street firms, polishing their resumes, and generally honing their academic and legal skills to my competitive disadvantage. Still, for a young law student contemplating a political future, it didn't seem like a bad education or a bad investment.

In my job as a Chamber manager I quickly learned that otherwise sane and entirely sensible people somehow became disoriented and irrational as tourists visiting an island. Though I am not sure anyone ever asked me what time the Mackinac Bridge swings over (as all dock porters claim they have been asked), I did get from inquiring tourists questions such as: Is the island surrounded by water? Is our American money good here? Can you get around the Island quicker on the shore road by going east or by going west? How far is it from here to America? One woman, looking out at the downtown harbor said to me, pointing to the left, "There's Lake Huron," and, pointing to the right, "And I know that's Lake Michigan. But where's the Straits of Magellan?"

Another time, a woman asked me where she might go to the bathroom. Thinking of the public restroom building just 50 feet behind our little Chamber of Commerce office, I

There must have been an Island clothing sale on men's sports coats, judging by the apparel of (front L-R) the author, Barry McGuire, my predecessor as Chamber manager, and Gov. John B. Swainson in this 1962 photo taken in front of Marquette Park. Swainson, a legless World War II veteran, served a single term, losing his re-election to George Romney just a few months after this photo was taken.

Hugh Downs and Barbara Walters on the set of *Today,* the show that came to Mackinac Island in 1963. They are flanked by Jack Lescoulie, left, who also made the trip, and newcaster Frank Blair, right, who remained as anchor back in the New York studios.

replied, "Right behind this building, Ma'am." Fatal error. Minutes later, peering out the back window of our office, I spied the woman busily squatting in the grass in the shadow of our back door.

In the summer of 1963 the nationally televised NBC *Today Show* chose Mackinac for a live two-hour two-day show. For the Island, it was a very big deal, the chance to garner a viewership of millions without having to spend a dime of our own. We envisioned a veritable cascade of additional tourists, an unprecedented boom in business. As Chamber manager, my job was to assist in making the many detailed local arrangements for the show's production.

Upon NBC's arrival on the Island my first task was to take *Today's* two stars and co-hosts, Barbara Walters and Hugh Downs, on a carriage ride to generally acquaint them with the Island, its geography, points of interest, and history. I soon discovered that Barbara Walters wanted to do all the talking. Every time I opened my mouth to describe this monument or point out that vista, Walters would interrupt with her own monologue. Occasionally, Downs would interject a brief comment, but Walters just kept on chattering. No matter how many times I tried to return the subject to what we were seeing, Walters would talk through or over me. I finally gave up and simply enjoyed the rest of the carriage ride in silence. As for Barbara Walters, she yakked all the way back to the barn.

For the most part, things went well on show day. Promptly at 7 a.m., July 21, 1963, *Today* opened with a shot of a long line of carriages coming down Grand Hotel hill. The producers then cut away to a very photogenic Dun Flanagan greeting passengers disembarking from an Arnold Line boat and exhorting them to "take the world famous buggy ride." The next sequence was to be that of blacksmith Dick Gimmel plying his horse-shoeing skills in the Carriage Tours barn and explaining how it was done.

It nearly didn't happen. Gimmel, a crusty, powerfully-built, talkative old-timer who always wore the top of his work shirts unbuttoned the better to reveal his thick white chest hair, suddenly suffered a severe case of stage fright. Thirty minutes before he was to go "live," he became tongue tied, his knees suddenly wobbly. The would-be star blanched. His collapse appeared imminent. Jack Chambers, who had been enlisted to make sure that Gimmel showed up that morning and prop him up if and when necessary, sprang into action. A jug of Old Grand Dad was quickly located, its contents quickly drained, and the star revived in the nick of time.

Dun Flanagan and Dick Gimmel, NBC later told me, had been the hits of the entire two hour show. Turns out we didn't need Barbara Walters anyway.

Each September, I journeyed to Harvard and a very different world, to return eagerly again to Mackinac the following June.

The Chamber manager accepts a stack of 1963 tourist inquiries from Postmaster Emerson Dufina.

Photo by Benjamin
Smiling Dennis Cawthorne, Secretary-Manager of the Chamber of Commerce, gladly accepts a batch of mail inquiries from Postmaster Emerson Dufina. Mr. Cawthorne predicts a "banner season" for Mackinac Island this year judging by the large number of inquiries received daily by the Chamber.

Sam McIntire was one of the three Chamber of Commerce board presidents I worked for as Chamber manager. McIntire, a state trooper was bodyguard for Gov. G. Mennen Williams.

Williams subsequently encouraged McIntire in the early 1950s to purchase the Island's then very modest Iroquois Hotel. The photogenic McIntire family was featured in a number of newspaper and magazine articles during my years as Chamber manager. Left to right: Martie, Margaret, Aaron, Mary Kay, Becki, Sam.

Robert Hughey, owner of the popular Little Bob's Restaurant, was mayor when I first came to the Island in 1960.

Ray Smith, Harrisonville resident, succeeded Hughey as mayor in the early 1960s. Smith was a local employed in MRA's maintenance department but was not necessarily an adherent of the organization.

Clemens Gunn, a retired Cleveland, Ohio stockbroker, was elected mayor not long after moving to the Island full-time in the late 1960s. Gunn's wife was a granddaughter of U.S. Supreme Court Justice William Day who maintained a home in the Annex.

Dr. Joseph Solomon became mayor in the mid-1960s. He essentially doubled as Island and MRA physician. An MRA adherent, he was one of the relatively few Islanders to bridge the MRA – community chasm.

THE CITY

The City of Mackinac Island's corporate boundaries are rather expansive ("all of Mackinac Island and Round Island . . . and the navigable waters adjacent . . . for the distance of one mile from the shorelines of said Islands"), according to the charter granted by the Michigan Legislature in 1899 and taking effect on March 20, 1900.

The City's real political jurisdiction, however, covers only a tiny fraction of that geographic area, making the municipality unique for what it doesn't govern. State law is very specific in providing that 83% of Mackinac's land area is exclusively governed by the Mackinac Island State Park Commission and subject only to its rules and ordinances. Anyone taking the shore road around the island would pass in and out of the City's jurisdiction, and be subject to its laws, at least ten times . . . and therefore in and out of the State Park, and be subject to its laws, an equal number of times. All of Round Island is federal property and thus not subject to city laws. The surrounding unpopulated one mile of water is essentially ungoverned. Viewed from that perspective, the City of Mackinac Island, as a municipal entity, controls perhaps only 10% of the area granted it by charter.

That all of this is not just an academic exercise was well-illustrated by a "bust" the City's police made for violation of the open container law in the early 1980s. Arrested was a well-known local property owner who also had recently served several terms as the elected prosecuting attorney of a neighboring northern Michigan county. The offense was consuming one or more beers in Marquette Park, just below the Fort, on a lazy summer afternoon. On City lands the charge might have stuck but, alas for the local gendarmes, there is no state park rule forbidding a quiet quaff on state park land. Case dismissed. (A few years later, the State Park amended its rules to prohibit open containers in Marquette Park but only within 75 feet of City land.) The moral of the story is that if you take a six pack on your next bike trip around the Island, make sure you are chugging your open beer in one of the ten stretches of M-185 that is within the State Park.

When I arrived in 1960 the mayor, elected then and now for a one-year term, was Robert Hughey, diminutive proprietor of the popular Little Bob's Restaurant. His six-member Board of Alderman, two elected each year for three-year terms, morphed at least in name into what is now popularly called the "City Council."

By the time I became Chamber manager, the Island had a new mayor, Ray Smith, a long-time Harrisonville resident who worked for MRA's maintenance department but who was not necessarily an MRA adherent. His successor, Island physician Joe Solomon, was an adherent and he served as mayor for several terms at the height of MRA's local influence. Then followed Clemens Gunn, a retired Cleveland, Ohio, stockbroker whose wife's ancestry included Justice of the United States Supreme Court William Day, the original owner of the Gunn home in the Annex. After Gunn there came Otto (Bud) Emmons, a Carriage Tours employee, who in office led the "Snowmobilers' Revolt" against the State Park Commission.

Through all of this, however, in 1960 and into the mid-1970s, city government was essentially archaic and slow to respond to change, even measured by the Island's horse and buggy standards. There were virtually no building and architectural rules. Some structures even into the 1970s were constructed with not so much as a building permit. Zoning was vague, a master plan non-existent. No rules controlled commercial signage, save for a ban on flashing neon signs. Garbage was burned in a public dump that the State threatened to close, the water and sewer systems limited and out of date. Public facilities, including the library, City Hall, and community center were cramped and in dire need of restoration. Tax assessing was non-professional and marked by rank favoritism. The only full-time city employees were one maintenance person and the chief of police, supplemented in the summer by three or four patrolmen. The fire department's single ancient truck and volunteer force was fortunately augmented by trucks and volunteers from the State Park and MRA.

None of this deterred colorful characters from being candidates for local office. Running for mayor in the late 1960s was a bushy-browed, stogie-chomping carriage driver by the name of Chester O'Brien who conducted his campaign, the *Detroit Free Press* reported, from a bar stool in Horn's Palm Café. He came close to winning, twice, but as local wags put it, "no cigar." Another mayoral contender, much later, was Larry Parel, a waiter, house painter, sometime maître d', accomplished story-teller, and raconteur. Of mixed ethnic heritage, his self-selected slogan "Elect the Jew in '92" failed to win him a majority at the polls. The next time out, he dropped the slogan for a new message which produced no better results in a re-match with the incumbent mayor. Still another mayoral candidate was undeterred by a recent conviction of safe-cracking.

Long winter days with short daylight hours sometimes encouraged City Council members to prepare for their late afternoon meetings by first getting well-fortified at Horn's Palm Café, then the Island's only year-round saloon. The foreseeable result on occasion produced some rollicking Council meetings, often attended by citizens eager for some comedy to get them through the Island's winter doldrums.

Presiding at one of her first meetings as the newly-elected mayor in 1975, a disgusted Margaret Doud summarily adjourned the session for reasons obvious to all in the audience. Council members got the message and never again under her reign did a Councilperson show up obviously intoxicated.

The earnest young mayor brought to local government a new purpose and seriousness to City business. Cautious but determined, for the next four decades she led and/or presided over badly needed changes. Zoning, planning, and architectural review were all greatly strengthened. With funding help from the federal government (thanks to U.S. Congressmen Bob Traxler and Bob Davis), a new library was built, the City Hall and community center renovated, and sewage, waste, and water treatment plants built. The positions of clerk, treasurer, DPW director, and assessor were made full or nearly full-time. Building codes and inspections were improved and the fire department far better equipped and trained. Police presence was greatly increased (some said too much so) and many other public improvements made.

As a member of the State Legislature and later as chairman of the State Park Commission, I deliberately stayed out of most affairs and issues of City Government, the better to concentrate my efforts and political capital in areas relevant to my own office. However, I did draft and push the City Council hard for passage of a sign control ordinance and an "anti-McDonald's" retail chain ban. The sign ordinance, though not as strong as I would have liked, represented a major step forward in saving downtown from clutter. My draft and passage of the "anti-McDonald's" ordinance came too late to stop a Starbucks but in time to prevent other "formula food" or similar retail operations from invading the community.

What would have happened in the community had Margaret Doud not been mayor for the past nearly forty years we cannot know. What we do know is that she contributed immensely, at considerable personal sacrifice, to the progress and sustainability of the Mackinac Island community by stitching together disparate local factions and interests in ways that few others could have.

A busy day on the Island ice bridge to St. Ignace, 2014, during the coldest, snowiest winter in decades.

WINTER

My first winter-time visit to Mackinac was on a cold, picture-perfect day in late January 1966. The sky was cobalt blue, the air crystal clear at a brittle 15 degrees. The previous night a heavy snow had fallen and the entire Island was cloaked in a deep, pristine mantel of white. If anything, the Island, locked in a vast expanse of ice, seemed more spectacular in winter than in summer.

I had come across the ice from St. Ignace by motor sleigh, an open cockpit on runners propelled by a large fan-like device mounted on its rear. Snowmobiles were still something of a novelty and forbidden in any event from operating on the Island. The motor sleigh, built from sundry spare parts, operated between the St. Ignace and Mackinac Island harbors "on call" and at the whim of its owners, Islanders Jim Perault and Ray O'Brien.

The number of winter-time visitors to the Island in those days were a handful at best and one "earned his spurs" and considerable respect in the eyes of Islanders if one was intrepid enough to make the three mile crossing from the mainland in the dead of winter. The only Island businesses open during my first winter was Doud's Grocery, the hardware store, post office, state liquor store, and Horn's Palm Café. At least the essentials had been covered, I noted.

My thoughts wandered back to my first summer on the Island when I inquired of a local what he did on the Island in winter. I never forgot his response, delivered without a trace of emotion or irony: "Get up in the morning, go to the post office, go to Horn's, go home, go to bed. Get up in the morning, go to the post office, go to Horn's, go home, go to bed." Other locals, when asked, would simply say that in the winter Islanders get ready for the next summer.

I had come that winter at the invitation of Jack Chambers whose friends had put together a "Life Begins at 40" birthday party in his honor. Needing a break from my first campaign for the state legislature, I was glad for the diversion. As it turned out, the party at Jack's Manure Manor lasted for the entire weekend and by Sunday I was ready for a retreat back across the Straits.

In those days, the 1960s, when Arnold Line stopped running for the season because of immovable ice, real isolation would set in. Air service was not always an alternative because the landing field atop the island was unpaved and ice in the downtown harbor not always solid enough to support a plane.

When the boats stopped, usually around January 5, the 450 or so Islanders hunkered down for a long winter. The pace even slowed to less than the clippity-clop lassitude of summer. Since there were no snow machines permitted on the Island, mobility within its land confines was decidedly limited. Provisions for the winter would be laid in well in advance, including plenty of cans of evaporated milk for the kids since there was no guarantee of a supply of fresh whole milk. Sides of beef were procured and canned goods of all kinds stocked in great volume. On occasion, stormy, wind-whipped weather or fog would prevent for days the replenishment of vital supplies and delivery of mail.

Inevitably, "Rock Fever" would set in and by March of each year Islanders were in the throes of what is locally known as *the mean season*. "Seeing the same people in the same snowmobile suits in the same bar telling the same stories will do that to a person," one Islander told me. Jack Chambers put it another way. "It's tough for a man to spend nearly six months in a place where the only thing you see a woman wearing in public is a snowmobile suit."

Wiser heads thus knew that the third month of the year was the time all sane people should make their one escape from an Island winter and this they did, to the east coast of Florida thru the 1970s and to the west coast in the years after.

In later years the old Village Inn was the Island's lone winter watering hole to be succeeded after a few winters by the Mustang. Within the old Village Inn a volleyball court was set up, low ceilings notwithstanding, to amuse winter patrons and stoke their competitive juices. At the Mustang, competition involving pitching empty beer cans into a barrel from a distant sitting position became the entertainment du jour until the management forbade the sport under pain of permanent banishment.

There was no punishment more cruel for local quaffers than to be barred from the Mustang in winter. The threat wasn't fully effective. Jack Chambers, defying management orders, was barred for the balance of one winter but set up his own informal "backdoor saloon" to entertain his friends in the rear of the closed Village Inn.

The end of the Island's snowmobile ban in 1973 had a profound impact on winter life. Locals marveled over the sense of freedom they felt being now able to zip over to St. Ignace for groceries, entertainment, or a beer. On the Island itself, older people were much more likely to get out of the house and go to a bingo game at the church or community hall. Typical was Helga Doud who used her machine into her 93rd year.

It was literally true that people, with their snowmachines, were more mobile than they were in the summer on their bicycles. Consequently, while the State Park Commission reluctantly acceded to the push for snowmobiles it took steps to limit their use and range. Essentially, the east half of the Island was closed to snowmobiles and dedicated to 40 miles of well-groomed cross country trails. Most of the main roads on the west half of the Island were kept open to the machines as was M-185 around the island.

To facilitate safe winter snowmobile passage to St. Ignace across the 3 miles of frozen Straits water, locals have for many years placed used Christmas trees at intervals as soon as ice conditions allowed. With approximately 150 snowmobiles based on the Island, and many more crossings by non-Islanders, the "ice bridge" in high season can carry an astounding amount of traffic. Local law enforcement authorities

The author on a vintage snowmobile on the frozen waters in front of Mission Point, 1966.

have never "approved" these crossings and indeed disappearance and death has not been a stranger. The Island's mailman, Lloyd St. Louis, went thru the ice with his dog team to a cold watery grave in 1937. In my fifty-four years I personally knew over a half dozen people who were lost in transit. When my (future) wife made her first trip across the ice with me in 1975 we rode as passengers with two Islanders who roared bucking and plunging over and through slush and watery holes. The next day most of the ice had moved out of that part of the Straits. I have often thought that we may have come closer to meeting our Eternal Maker that night than we knew.

For a brief winter or two in the 1990s, the Tourism Bureau coaxed along the idea of the Island being a winter tourism destination. The idea soon succumbed to the reality of inconsistent and erratic weather that too often frustrated tourists' travel plans for going to and from the Island. One winter, that of 2011-12, saw virtually no snow, but in the winter of 2014, it was possible to walk onto the roof of our cottage from snowdrifts massed along its side. In 1990, a full-blown St. Patrick's Day party attended by over 50 people was staged on the solid ice of the Straits, a mile and a half from land in any direction. Complete with large portable grills, full bar, beer kegs, televisions, gigantic speakers with blaring music, it was hard to believe that, by the calendar, spring was only four days away.

Islander Sonny Therrian with sleigh on Mahoney Avenue, 1966

This motor-sleigh took me across the ice from St. Ignace for my first winter visit to Mackinac, 1966, piloted by Jim (Sperry) Perault.

Taking out the Mustang pool table became an Island rite of passage every spring. Above, Grand Hotel musicians led by leader and clarinetist Bob Snyder and local octogenarian Agnes Shine (far right), salute the end of winter and literally make space inside the Mustang to accommodate the crowds of summer.

Five members of the Michigan House of Representatives, obviously in summer break mode, pay an impromptu visit to Chief Eagle Eye's residence in July 1969. L-R, Rep. Joe Swallow of Alpena, Rep. Hal Ziegler of Jackson, Rep. David Serotkin of Mt. Clemens, Rep. Bob Traxler of Bay City, and the author, then of Manistee and representing the 98th House district.. Later that day, Rep. Ziegler would find himself in the Mackinac Island jail. Traxler would go on to become a member of the U.S. Congress and still later a member of the State Park Commission. Swallow became a Michigan circuit judge.

Legislative Days: All Work and No Play . . .

From 1967 to 1979 as a state legislator, I immersed myself in major state-wide issues and rose thru the ranks to become by 1974 the Republican House leader. Though my district was 200 miles downstate and my first allegiance was necessarily to my district I still had numerous opportunities to accomplish some positive things for the Island through the legislative process.

In 1968 I co-sponsored a bill to cut tolls on the Mackinac Bridge from $3.25 each way to $1.50. With bi-partisan support, the measure was aimed at stimulating traffic to the tourist-dependent Straits area communities including the Island. It passed and tolls remained at that low level into the 21st century.

Another initiative was early 1970s legislation to allow the newly-renovated Island House Hotel to sell alcoholic beverages in its dining room. The hotel was (and is) the property of the Mackinac State Park Commission and, as state property, generally forbidden from such activity absent specific legislative authorization. Fudge mogul Harry Ryba had leased the dilapidated, tax-reverted hotel in 1970, once the home of MRA, on condition that he totally renovate the property. To sweeten the deal, the Commission threw in 150 bike licenses and a promise to get him a liquor license. The southern half of my five county legislative district was relatively conservative on liquor issues, and as a young legislator I did not want to be too far "out front" on such matters. My desire to do good for Mackinac won out on this occasion, however, and I consented to be chief sponsor of the House bill authorizing the license. My legislation to help the Commission and Ryba started to sail swiftly through the House.

Then the bar owners' association (now the Michigan Licensed Beverage Association) entered the picture. Suddenly everything changed. Unhappy with my "no" votes on most of their other issues, MLBA vowed to block the Mackinac bill in retaliation. Reluctantly, I stepped aside and the bill moved forward as a Senate-initiated measure. The three Senate sponsors, Sens. L. Harvey Lodge (R-Waterford), Oscar Bouwsma (R-Muskegon), and Stanley Novak (D-Detroit), promptly recognized a good thing. For the next three years (until Lodge's and Bouwsma's defeat in 1974) they made annual summer trips to "inspect the implementation" of their legislation and stick the Island House with nights of free lodging and days of copious food and drink.

It was a red-letter day for northern Michigan and Mackinac Island when Gov. George Romney signed legislation in 1968 cutting the Mackinac Bridge toll to $1.50 each way. Present at the signing were the bill's sponsors (L-R): Rep. Joe Swallow of Alpena, Sen. Thomas Schweigert of Petoskey, Robert W. Davis of St. Ignace, Dominic Jacobetti of Negaunee, Charles Varnum of Manistique, and the author. Jacobetti would be instrumental over a decade later in the State Park Commission engaging former Senator Stanley Novak as its lobbyist.

In 1974 Bill Doyle, Jack Chambers, and I (then in my fourth House term), put together the first Friends of Mackinac reception for Lansing's political decision-makers. We hosted eight legislators over dinner and a liberal supply of cocktails. The original idea was to keep the list of invitees small, highly selective, and therefore highly coveted. Each year the number of politician-invitees grew, however, and we began to add other Island business and community leaders as hosts. Within a few years, after I had ceased being a member of the legislature, our guests numbered over 50 and hosts over 15. In 2014, we celebrated the 42nd annual convening of Friends of Mackinac. Now one of the oldest and most anticipated

Lansing political receptions, it was attended by 150 movers-and-shakers from all three branches of government. The purpose of these gatherings, of course, was to build political good will and promote governmental actions of direct benefit to the Island. That it was done over cocktails and conversational banter, without a "hard sell" or overt pleadings, made our lobbying efforts for Mackinac that much more effective. The "ask" and the "hard sell" could always come later.

Not everyone was capable of grasping that notion. Dr. Eugene Petersen, a respected historian and able state park director but something of a prima donna in political matters, sniffed in his book *Inside Mackinac*, "I had been invited to attend (Friends of Mackinac) one year but found the session amounted to little more than a dinner and drinking session with no formal agenda."

In fact, Friends of Mackinac's efforts over the years met with resounding success, not just for Island businesses and local government but for the state park as well. Generous state aid for the Island medical center, Straits Hospital, school, and federal money for sewer and water systems have all been the direct result of the Friends receptions. The post-Labor Day school start, Pure Michigan, state park capital outlay and operations, and countless other legislative endeavors have also been impacted by the good will engendered by the Island hosts.

One of the highlights of my earliest legislative days was the annual trip of the House Judiciary Committee to attend the convention of the Michigan Prosecuting Attorneys Association at Grand Hotel. After the 1968 convention, the Prosecutors sent the Clerk of the House a bill for all the wine our members drank at the Association's evening banquet. The total number of bottles consumed, and the attendant cost charged to the House, sent the Clerk into near shock, and there were soon revisions in legislative rules regarding such matters.

That summer committee members decided, at my suggestion unfortunately, to have some fun with one of our members, Rep. Hal Ziegler of Jackson. Ziegler, having too much time on his hands during the Prosecutors convention, had tried talking a young Island female employee into joining him downtown for a drink. To accomplish this, he knocked on the door of the girl's rooming house, got rejected, returned, persevered, and was again rejected. This time a security guard appeared and threatened to have Ziegler arrested for trespass.

Hearing Ziegler's tale, we decided to take matters a bit further. In a move unthinkable these days, I paid a visit to Police Chief Jim Ryerse and convinced him to prepare an arrest warrant signed by the Island's justice of the peace, the nonexistent, totally fictional John P. Donniker. By pre-arrangement, as our Judiciary Committee members, lawyers all, sat

around a table enjoying drinks at the old Village Inn, there appeared an MIPD cop seeking "a Hal Ziegler." Ziegler bit, the warrant was handed him, and ten minutes later he was behind bars at the Mackinac Island jail.

After about forty-five minutes and several more fortifying rounds, our legislative contingent arose from its VI table and trooped off to the jail. The prisoner was not a happy person. We told him we would get him a good lawyer ("None of you guys, I hope," Ziegler said tellingly), try to shield him from a hungry news media which, we confided, were already on the story of his arrest, and campaign for him door to door now that his re-election campaign – just three months off – was in obvious jeopardy. At times we thought Ziegler was about to burst into tears. Unable to contain ourselves and feeling genuinely sorry for the colleague we had so effectively duped, we finally came clean. Ziegler did not speak to us for a month.

A far happier time on Mackinac during my legislative years was my marriage to Cynthia Knoth on August 21, 1976 at historic St. Anne's Church. Our reception at Grand Hotel and post-reception at the old Village Inn were events remembered to this day by invitees, among them Gov. Bill Milliken. Our honeymoon? Mackinac Island, of course.

Send in the Clowns

One of the highlights of the Island's annual Lilac Festival parade is always the appearance of the Scottville Clown Band. No parade entry ever creates more "buzz," fun, and pure entertainment than this downstate musical aggregation that was formed over one hundred years ago and today performs all over the Great Lakes area.

They made their first appearance on the Island in 1968 when I arranged to have them make the 400-mile round trip north. Scottville was in my legislative district, nearly all of the musicians were constituents and the Lilac Parade, which in my past Chamber days I had helped organize, badly needed something to spice it up. Perfect combination.

Well, almost. Arriving in late morning, by early afternoon one of the band members lingering too long in an Island watering hole, refused to quell his wailing saxophone, and was arrested for disturbing the peace. Band members bailed him out and the show went on. Later, the charges were quietly dropped. Meantime, I had forgotten to tell Bill Beardsley, my successor as Chamber manager and an assistant Michigan State University athletic director most of the year, that the band expected a $2,000 stipend for its performance. Beardsley recovered from his shock, scrounged up the necessary funds from the Chamber's meager treasury and, as they say, "the band played on."

It was several years before the band returned for another Lilac Day performance but when they did it was for an unbroken string of nearly 30 consecutive years and counting.

The Scottville Clown Band tunes up for its first Island appearance, June 1968.

State Park Commissioner and East Bluff resident Jim Dunnigan, along with a number of other locals, served as an extra in several scenes of the 1979 making of *Somewhere in Time*.

Actor Christopher Reeve leans out a gazebo, pulled by a dray and team of horses, greeting the crowd at the annual Lilac Parade.

Somewhere in Time

One of the Island's most memorable events during my years was the 1979 filming of the movie *Somewhere in Time*. Over an eight week period during May and June of that year, the Island was a beehive of activity for the making of the film which starred Christopher Reeve, Jane Seymour, and Christopher Plummer. Each had already made their mark in the movies: Reeve as *Superman,* Plummer in *Sound of Music*, and Seymour in myriad productions.

Somewhere in Time, based on Richard Matheson's novel *Bid Time Return*, was the story of a man who falls in love with a photo of a woman he sees in his hotel room and who, through sheer will power, transports himself back to the year 1912. As an historical romance the plot was well suited to Mackinac's Victorian setting.

Looking for a suitable site and first inclined to the Hotel Coronado in San Diego, the producers learned of Grand Hotel and Mackinac Island. The Grand, however, was already nearly fully booked for the summer and appeared out of the running because it could not provide rooms needed by the production's cast and crew. Grand Hotel president Dan Musser dispatched sales representatives to California who told producer Stephen Deutsch and director Jeannot Szwarc that Grand could still be available as a filming site and that housing accommodations were available at the Inn on Mackinac (the former MRA property). When the two learned that the latter facility had a sound stage equal to or better than anything in Hollywood, their interest peaked. Deutsch and Szwarc flew to the Island in early April, scouted the community, and concluded a deal with Musser to film on Mackinac.

Production at Grand Hotel proved a challenge. Ballroom scenes could only be shot post-dinner and pre-breakfast, i.e. late night to early morning. Each night Grand's dining room was transformed with massive movements of furniture. Woodwork was darkened with stage paint, and chandeliers, drapes, and music stands altered. Rugs, potted palms, and curio cabinets were added to complete a 1912 look and feel.

Motor vehicles were given special permits by the City to accommodate their use as changing rooms and equipment haulers, usually well out of public view. Production sites

away from Grand Hotel included Round Island, the MRA soundstage, the Island school, downtown, and the Loretta Dennany residence in the Mission.

Locals gaped at the filming (I was surprised at the very petite dimensions of Jane Seymour). Some were hired as "extras" for $25 a day. They soon discovered the work wasn't easy: nearly every scene was shot and re-shot many times over and Grand Hotel ballroom scenes were filmed well after midnight. The stars of the show won the favor of locals by often mingling with them at filmings and afterward. At one late-night outdoor filming bats whizzed around the actors and in the final product one can be seen fluttering at the edges of a shot near the Island school. After each day's work, film was sent off to California for review and editing.

When at last the finished movie premiered at Grand Hotel in a special showing for locals, it seemed likely the film was not destined for greatness. Heaviest applause from the audience came when familiar locals in Victorian attire appeared on the screen. But that was not the end of the story. *Somewhere in Time* eventually became a cult favorite with a huge following on late night cable television. It became one of the most "repeated plays" on television and one major station, WGN-TV of Chicago, even featured it non-stop on a Valentine's Day 25 years after its filming.

Within a few years after the movie's release, Grand Hotel was featuring *Somewhere in Time* weekends and attracting hundreds of period-dress aficionados. Jane Seymour returned several times for the events, but not Christopher Reeve whose life was cut short by a tragic riding accident that paralyzed and eventually claimed him. *Somewhere in Time* remains an icon and symbol of Grand Hotel and Mackinac Island.

Christopher Reeve takes time out to cruise the Straits with (L-R) Ron Dufina, Ron Tomlinson, and Jack Chambers, captain of the "I Ain't Skairt," May 1979.

Grand Hotel
The Woodfill Era

My first introduction to Grand Hotel came in early June 1960, just three weeks before I arrived on the Island for my summer job with Carriage Tours. My parents were regular readers of the *Saturday Evening Post,* the nation's foremost popular magazine, and I was drawn to its five page spread on the hotel and its imposing owner, W. Stewart Woodfill.

I was understandably fascinated by the *Post's* description of Woodfill:

"The locals all know that the enigmatic Great Man of the Grand Hotel is more than a hotel keeper. When he moves, they jump. When he speaks, they listen. And when he thumps his walking stick, the heavens appear to crash and miracles descend. The local Indians call him Chief Walkum Stick. Most people call him 'Mister' Woodfill or 'sir.' He summons his guests to dinner with a yachtsman's whistle. He rides erect and lordly in a vis-a-vis carriage with hackney team and top-hatted, red-coated coachmen. As he transports himself about his dominion, the grapevine passes the word: 'Here he comes, the old gink with the stick.' Woodfill, a whimsical, self-made millionaire of sixty-three, is a rare phenomenon in America, a sort of feudal prince. His realm, Mackinac Island. A man of sturdy build, courtly manner and definitive mind, he never has wavered in his love for fastidiously tailored but long-out-of-style double-breasted sport jackets, always complemented with a gentleman's straight walking-stick, not a cane."

W. Stewart Woodfill

Francis Stockbridge, Kalamazoo millionaire and Annex property owner, was one of the first to conceive of a Mackinac hotel on a grand scale. To that end he purchased one of the premier properties on the West Bluff high over the waters of Lake Huron. Elected to the United States Senate

a few years later in 1885 and thus engaged, he kept alive his dream of a hotel on the site by selling it to a conglomerate of railroad and steamship companies. The companies needed a "destination" for their patrons. A hotel in the style then sweeping Europe and major American resorts would fill that bill. The hotel's builder, Charles Caskey, completed his work in just over three months using 300 workers, a million and a half feet of lumber, and not a single power tool. When Grand Hotel opened to great fanfare on July 10, 1887, its 200 plus rooms could be had for $3 to $5 a night during its 8-week season. Despite its opulence and early fame, however, Grand Hotel soon proved to be a money-losing investment and at one point its owners actually contemplated tearing it down and selling it for the value of its lumber.

W. Stewart Woodfill had come to Grand Hotel as a 23-year-old desk clerk and soon moved up to the position of hotel manager. When the hotel's owner, Logan Ballard, died, Woodfill scraped together funds to buy Grand Hotel with two other investors. When the arrangement didn't work to his satisfaction, at age 31 in 1927 he sold out to the others. Within a few years, weighed down by heavy debt and crushed by the Great Depression, the hotel went into receivership. When it was put up for auction by its creditors in 1933, there was only one bidder. W. Stewart Woodfill was now the sole owner of Grand Hotel.

Even under Woodfill, Grand Hotel struggled financially for the first few years. On the night of July 11, 1939 there were exactly eleven overnight guests and a paid staff of 400 employees. But Woodfill saved Grand Hotel through sheer hard work and his unerring sense of publicity. 1940 was a banner year, 1941 nearly so. Then came World War II and discretionary travel ground to a halt. Following the war, however, his public relations talents went into overdrive, culminating in the 1946-47 filming on Mackinac of Metro-Goldwyn-Mayer's *This Time for Keeps* starring Esther Williams and Jimmy Durante. The Woodfill legend grew and Grand Hotel prospered. He expanded his public role by successfully pushing, with others, construction of the Mackinac Bridge and, as we shall see, taking on the chairmanship of the State Park Commission to lead the way in refurbishing and revitalizing its priceless historic properties.

The Musser family, 1987. Seated, L-R, Robin Musser Agnew, Amelia Musser, Margaret Musser Cunningham. Standing, L-R, James Agnew, R. D. Musser, R. D. Musser III.

Dan and Amelia Musser, shown here in 2012, were responsible for transforming Grand Hotel's interior into a true place of beauty after they took ownership in 1979.

Grand Hotel
The Musser Era

In the year I became Chamber of Commerce manager, 1962, Woodfill's nephew, R. Daniel Musser Jr., became president of Grand Hotel. Dan Musser had started his career as a cashier in 1950 during a summer off from Dartmouth College. During the ensuing decade he steadily worked his way up Grand Hotel's management ladder. The relationship between Woodfill and his young nephew was generally formal and in later years often stressful, at least for the latter, as Woodfill became increasingly eccentric and reclusive.

A major turning point for Grand Hotel occurred in 1962 when Musser as president, accompanied by his wife Amelia, visited Grand Hotel of Clear Point, Alabama. They came away greatly impressed by that hotel's furnishings, artwork, tasteful décor, and "warmth of style married to fundamental beauty." Woodfill, whose taste in the Victorian hotel incongruously ran to plastic and vinyl, resisted change and its accompanying expenditure of money. For nearly 15 years the Mussers waited patiently for a more receptive Woodfill.

Finally, in 1976 the Mussers convinced him that the time had come for extreme change—a structural shoring up of the hotel and a thorough renovation of both exterior and interior. For the latter, the Mussers called in Carleton Varney, a renowned New York interior designer with an affinity for summer places. They agreed that they wanted a true "summer place" with no two guest rooms alike, and that new colors and vintage furniture were a key. When finished, Varney's makeover had transformed Grand Hotel into the tasteful, beautiful place the Mussers had long envisioned. Locals and overnight guests were thrilled by the final product.

Woodfill, distant, cantankerous, and ill, decided his time had come to leave Mackinac forever. I recall the day he did, September 19, 1978. Accompanied by Dan Musser, he waited for a Shepler ferry across the street from the old Village Inn. At one point, the weather being somewhat inclement, the two walked into the Village Inn for a brief word with Jack Chambers, its proprietor. I spotted the pair but did not have the opportunity to speak with them. Only Dan Musser knew that Woodfill was leaving Mackinac for the last time. He wanted to leave unannounced, he confided to Musser, "because he wished to avoid painful

farewells." Once aboard the departing Shepler's boat, he never looked back. It was only the next spring that locals learned that Woodfill, now ensconced in his Scottsdale, Arizona home, would never return. He passed away March 4, 1984.

A strange footnote to his departure occurred the following summer. The year before, Woodfill decided to put the hotel on the market, somehow afraid that his property could yet go broke after the huge capital expenditures made the previous year. Dan Musser offered to buy it, and to Woodfill's amazement, found the capital resources to do so. Woodfill accepted Musser's offer. On July 21, 1979, however, the Island newspaper, *The Town Crier* carried a front page story:

> "*W. Stewart Woodfill Gives His Nephew R. Daniel Musser His Grand Hotel, His Home, and His Island Properties*"
>
> W. Stewart Woodfill has presented as a gift to his nephew, R. Daniel Musser, his Grand Hotel, his home on Lake Shore Drive, the house in which Mr. and Mrs. Musser live, and all the other Island property belonging to Woodfill, the gift's worth estimated to comprise eight digits… Mr. Woodfill asked that Mr. Musser be apprised of his gift through this announcement…"

The "announcement," however, did not comport with the facts, but not through any fault of *The Town Crier*. Grand Hotel's ownership passed to Dan Musser through a straight forward commercial transaction, not as a gift. Why Woodfill chose to state otherwise is a Mackinac mystery second only to the Lacey murder.

Free at last to direct Grand Hotel in every respect, Dan and Amelia Musser set about their task with renewed vigor. A long list of improvements to the hotel ensued: expanded gardens, additional rooms, a cupola bar, another golf course, an athletic club, and on-going changes to virtually every room and facility of the hotel. All of this was undertaken in the years after 1979 and was in addition to their acquiring properties outside of Grand Hotel: ownership of the Woods Restaurant and Gatehouse (formerly the French Outpost) and agreements to operate the Fort Tea Room and Cawthorne's Village Inn.

As owners of Grand Hotel, the Mussers moved their family to Michigan year-round in the late 1970s, opened new winter offices in Lansing, and greatly increased the hotel's marketing efforts in the entire Great Lakes region. Dan became Chairman of the Michigan Lodging Association and later chaired the Michigan Travel Commission. On the Island, Dan saw the urgent need for upgrading the City's ancient and decrepit infrastructure. He

accepted the Mayor's appointment to chair the Board of Public Works, and he plunged himself into the arduous task of securing funds for a new sewer system, water lines, and solid waste treatment. By the 1980s those tasks were completed, along with a repaving of virtually all City streets and sidewalks.

Though I could not claim any personal relationship with Woodfill, I had many business and social interchanges with Musser going back as far as 1962. He was a hard-headed businessman who paid meticulous personal attention to his guests. He was also scrupulously fair, congenial, and generous to the community. It often amazed me the number of local fundraisers and charities that Grand Hotel helped underwrite. Locals, although always respectful, felt at ease in Dan Musser's company, a contrast from Woodfill's imperious style. Musser's annual season-ending appreciation party for locals further cemented the bond between the community and Grand Hotel.

Early in the 21st century, R.D. Musser III, "Danny" to some, became President of Grand Hotel. The elder Dan became Chairman of the Board, then retired more or less completely in 2012. Dan III was possessed of many of his father's best attributes and my relationship with him always highly positive. When the new Mackinac Island Convention and Visitors Bureau was formed, Dan III became president and, though not a hotelier myself, I agreed to become vice-chair. The young Musser, like his father, chose well in marriage, when Marlee Brown, daughter of former State Park Commissioner Meg Brown and Paul, and a granddaughter of Prentiss Brown, became his wife and tastefully interjected her artistic talents into Grand Hotel. Mimi Musser Cunningham, daughter of Dan and Amelia, also was a major part of Grand Hotel's management team, along with key participants John Hulett and Ken Hayward. This team led Grand Hotel to its greatest years ever. In 2012, I and many other locals were on hand to help the venerable institution celebrate its 125th anniversary.

Three generations of Musser gentlemen: R.D. Musser Jr., R.D. Musser III, and R.D. ("Quatro") Musser IV.

A gathering of the "old guard" at Grand Hotel's 125th birthday party, July 2012. L-R, former Gov. James Blanchard, former Attorney General Frank Kelley, former Gov. William Milliken, State Park Commission chairman Dennis Cawthorne, and former Gov. John Engler.

Island deputy sheriff (and future mayor) Otto "Bud" Emmons hands a citation for driving a motor vehicle onto the Island to the Canadian who came ashore in an "aqua-car." The intrepid operator put in at St. Ignace and plowed five miles through the Straits of Mackinac to reach "terra firma" at Mackinac. In fact, this 1963 photo was a staged event (by the Chamber of Commerce's enterprising young manager) and the driver never faced the Island's justice of the peace.

Saying "Neigh" to the Horseless Carriage

That Mackinac Island bans automobiles is of course well known. Indeed, it is one of the community's claims to fame and arguably its greatest attraction.

Less well known is the struggle it's been over the years to keep the ban intact. In 1898, after the first horse-spooking contraption arrived on the island, city fathers voted an immediate ban, motivated as much by a desire to protect the carriage business as by genuine safety concerns. In 1901 the State Park Commission followed suit by banning automobiles in its jurisdiction, although it was not put officially into state law until much later.

In 1926 State Park Superintendent Frank Kenyon, seeking to increase tourist traffic, obtained funds for building a dock at British Landing designed to receive automobiles that would arrive by state ferry. Kenyon's plan also called for constructing a parking garage opposite the dock where owners could leave their vehicles and proceed into town by horse and carriage. Service to the dock began on September 7, 1928, but although carrying over 700 passengers in its one month of operation, no automobiles made the trip. Before the 1929 season began, the Kenyon scheme died a quiet death. The land for the auto park opposite the British Landing dock remains a cleared field to this day.

The onset of the Great Depression, however, soon revived talk of allowing cars on Mackinac. Gov. Frank Fitzgerald, in residence at the Captain's Quarters during the summer of 1935, made a "tentative suggestion that the ban against automobiles be lifted . . . and (their) use be permitted on a limited scale." To reverse the Island's desperate lack of tourists that summer, Fitzgerald and others suggested a wide, paved highway around the Island which would allow state ferries already carrying motor vehicles between Mackinaw City and St. Ignace to make the Island a port of call. He also suggested reviving Kenyon's plan of an auto park near the British Landing dock. Joining the fray, former State Highway Commissioner Grover Dillman proposed a new two lane highway for the Island that "would be one of the most beautiful in the world."

At about the same time, advocates for a bridge across the Straits of Mackinac came up with a new variation on a dream that had existed since the late 19th century, and it, too, involved bringing cars to the Island. Their suggestion was a series of bridges that would link Cheboygan to Bois Blanc Island, Bois Blanc Island to Round Island, Round Island to Mackinac Island, and Mackinac—via the shore road—to St. Ignace. In the end the plans to build an auto highway on the Island died a quiet death.

Along the way, however, there have been some notable violations of the auto ban. Commander E. M. Tellefson, owner of a house at the northwest edge of the Island, but employed as a radio operator high on the Island's interior, had openly defied the auto ban for years. In 1933 he was at last arrested by the City marshal and hauled before the Island's Justice of the Peace. He was given a choice of a $25 fine or 25 days in jail. Tellefson appealed his conviction to the Mackinac County Circuit Court. The State, taking no chances, brought in a battery of high profile attorneys, including the venerable Prentiss M. Brown, to secure the conviction. Remnants of Tellefson's violating vehicle remained on his Point Aux Pins property into the 21st century.

In 1955 Moral Re-Armament (MRA) got around the ban by receiving "emergency permission" from the City to haul tons of gravel to a construction site at Mission Point. The State Park Commission, goaded by Bill Doyle, temporarily an ex-commissioner, sought an injunction to stop the trucks from crossing state lands. MRA agreed to haul the remaining 1,000 tons of gravel by teams of horses and the suit was dropped with the ban largely intact. Today both the City and State have relaxed the ban on dump trucks, bull dozers, and similar vehicles providing operations are confined to construction projects carried out between October 15 and May 1.

Surprisingly, even W. Stewart Woodfill, owner of Grand Hotel, tinkered with the idea of throwing the auto ban overboard. In the year I arrived on the island, he arranged for a quiet survey of Island visitors to get their reaction to "quiet and clean motorized transportation" as an alternative to horses. Woodfill never revealed the results of his survey.

The next major challenge to the motor vehicle ban came later in the 1960s. Gasoline powered vehicles which ran on tracks and moved easily over snow were made to order for Mackinac Islanders who saw for the first time that they could live on the Island and be mobile. Since 1945 a few islanders had been using motor sleighs—essentially a cockpit on runners propelled by a small airplane motor and a propeller. Snowmobiles, first in popular usage in the 1960s, were seen as a more comfortable alternative. Soon, despite the city and state ban on motor vehicles, snowmobiles were zipping in winter months all over the Island. Many residents complained that the high-pitched whine of their engines and their exhaust disrupted the winter peace, but a referendum at the City's April 1968 election approved their usage in the City. The State Park Commission, however, reaffirmed its ban on state lands and the stage was set for a showdown.

The next winter, Mayor Otto "Bud" Emmons led a parade of 50 snowmobiles past Marquette Park, up Mission Hill, and onto State Park grounds opposite the Fort in an open show of defiance. The Commission then tried a compromise that allowed only Harrisonville residents to follow a single road to the lakeshore and thence over the ice to the mainland but that was struck down in court as discriminatory vis-a-vis other Island residents. Bowing to the inevitable, the Commission in the fall of 1972 approved issuing temporary permits to local residents to traverse a limited number of specified roads.

City councilman Frank Bloswick Sr. had a graphic description of the machines which gave the Islanders their new sense of winter freedom: "You have to be a wizard or a mechanic with the constitution of a lumberjack to operate those things . . . but now in winter I can at least take my wife out to dinner."

Forty years later, the Commission still annually approves blanket permits to local residents for winter snowmobiles as a "temporary" measure for promotion of "health, safety, education, and work convenience." Over two hundred snowmobiles are now permitted for operation on the Island. Technically, non-residents are not allowed to bring their machines onto the Island but the ban is largely ignored.

It is perhaps ironic that on this island which bans motor vehicles, there is a state highway. M-185 is the 8.3 mile road that encircles the island, and it received its designation as a state highway in the early 1950s when the State Park Commission was scratching for ways to pass some of its maintenance costs onto other state agencies. The legislature bought into the plan, and the Michigan Department of Transportation to this day pays for the road's maintenance and upkeep.

By 1999, M-185 was clearly in need of re-building. As Commission chair I approached the director of the State Transportation Commission and told him we needed a major fix. "Fat chance" was the essence of his reply as he recited a litany of his department's own financial needs and unfinished projects. Undeterred, I pressed our case with key legislators and the Governor's office. When I was done, I got a call from the Transportation director. "You'll have your money," he said abruptly, and within weeks the re-building project was underway. When it was finished, nearly the entire 8.3 miles was widened, elevated, and given a new drainage system. M-185, safer than ever, may be the only state highway in America that has never recorded an auto fatality.

Louie "The Thief" Deroshia in 1965 brought his own vehicle to the horse and buggy island. Deroshia's Mustang was ordered to be hitched to a team of horses if it was going to leave the dock. J.D. "Dun" Flanagan is at far right. Police chief Dale Gallagher scratches his head and State trooper Arlie Brouwer seems to say "what next?" as they contemplate the scene. In the far background, Straits of Mackinac, with a thousand passenger capacity, rests in port.

Local residents opposed to the State Park Commission's ban on snowmobiles hold a protest parade, 1969. After three more years of wrangling, a reluctant State Park Commission finally yielded in late 1972 and allowed a "temporary" usage of selected, limited Island roads that remains the rule well into the 21st century.

Invasion of the "Carhartts." Each morning a small army of construction workers ride the first boat from St. Ignace to work on the Island. When newcomers to the Island decide they can do better by hiring their own crews from downstate, the fun begins. Carhartt is the favored, and signature, brand of the workers' outer clothing.

If You Build It They Will Come

Take it from me, anyone contemplating a building project on the Island must consider the following: the place poses construction obstacles of a kind found almost nowhere else. I know. I built (or, more precisely, contracted to have built) six different residential and commercial structures on the Island during a 25-year span from 1973 to 1998.

Consider labor costs. There being only two or three locally-based tradesmen or construction crews, it is usually necessary to hire a St. Ignace-based crew. By long tradition, workers expect to be paid portal-to-portal, resulting in the following typical work day:

7:30 a.m. - 8:00 a.m.   Ride the boat from St. Ignace, pay commencing at boat's departure
8:00 a.m. -8:30 a.m.   Peddle bike 1, 2, or 3 miles to construction site
8:30 a.m. – 10 a.m.   Work
10 a.m. – 10:15 a.m.   Coffee Break
10:15 a.m. – 12 noon   Work
12 noon – 12:30 p.m.   Lunch
12:30 p.m. – 2:15 p.m. Work
2:15 p.m. – 2:30 p.m.   Coffee Break
2:30 p.m. – 4:00 p.m.   Work
4:00 p.m. – 4:30 p.m.   Peddle bike back to boat dock
4:30 p.m. – 5:00 p.m.   Ride boat back to St. Ignace, pay ending when the boat docks

Total work time in a 9 hour pay day: 6 hours. Put another way: labor cost in any single day is 33-⅓ % higher than at the normal mainland job site. Add transportation costs not incurred at mainland sites: ferry tickets for workers; freight costs from the mainland; horse-drawn freight from boat to job site. Total additional cost of Island construction: 40% over same job performed on the mainland.

The solution? As any fool can see, it's obvious. Hire your own crew from back home downstate, rent a year-round apartment for them and bring them north for the duration of your project.

Here's how it really works. (And if you think anything below is fictional or exaggerated, I assure you that at various times over the years these things really happened.)

Day 1 – City issues building permit for project. Work begins.

Day 4 – Project delayed pending unexpected mandatory archeological study of the site to determine if Native American bones or relics present.

Day 6 – After additional delay due to non-availability of Native American inspectors, tentative approval given to commence excavation. Work commences.

Day 10 – City of Mackinac Island halts work due to plan revisions requiring Planning Commission approval.

Day 14 – Next meeting of Planning Commission scheduled, for two weeks from now.

Days 23-27 – Work crew, inactive for two weeks, spends "down-time" getting drunk at one of two bars open on the Island this time of the year.

Day 28 – Planning Commission OKs revised plans; project proceeds.

Days 29-32 – Crew too hungover to function, excavation at a stand still.

Day 33 – Work resumes.

Day 35 – Equipment breakdown; parts ordered from downstate; work on hold.

Day 38 – Parts arrive from mainland; wrong ones; must be returned; work still on hold.

Day 41 – New parts arrive; excavation proceeds.

Day 44 – Excavation complete; work moves to next phase.

Day 47 – City council decides, for obscure reasons, that City Building Inspector shouldn't have issued a building permit; police are dispatched to retrieve permit and lock it in City Hall safe; work stops.

Days 48-52 – Owner hires attorney, incurs 40 hours of charges at attorney's top hourly rate

Day 53 – Upon City Attorney's advice, Council relents and returns building permit to owner; work resumes.

Day 59 – Project owner cited by City for not having procured "off-Island business" license; work halted, fine paid, work resumed.

Day 65 – Ice in Straits too thick for freight boat to transport additional building materials but not thick enough to haul over the ice; work halted.

Day 68 – Three of crew arrested for drunk and disorderly fight with locals; remanded to jail; project owner springs for bail, attorney, fine, and court costs.

Day 71 – Contact made with Great Lakes Air Service to determine feasibility of flying building supplies to Island; determined that flying round-the-clock for 2 weeks straight might yield enough material for 4 days work.

Day 72 – Workers placed on unemployment pending breakup of ice estimated to be ten weeks hence. Before leaving Island workers accidentally turn heat up instead of down in rented apartment.

Day 144 – Project owner gets bill for $2,000, cost of electric heat for 10 weeks in the vacant employee apartment.

Day 146 – Freight boat makes its first Spring run; workers return, work resumes, apartment heat turned down.

Day 151 – Workers decide to take weekend break from Island; fly off.

Days 153-155 – Workers unable to return to Island, stuck in St. Ignace because passenger boats not yet running and snow squalls shut down St. Ignace and Mackinac Island airports.

Day 156 – Workers return, work resumes.

Day 161 – Work put on hold pending arrival of dray carrying materials needed for next phase; draymen, in sympathy with locals not hired for the job, engage in "silent sabotage," old but much-used means of slowing deliveries to non-favored parties.

Day 163 – Brown-wrapped package discreetly slipped to dray driver ensures future timely dray deliveries.

Days 164-179 – Work proceeds; amazing progress made.

Day 180 – Indian bones unexpectedly discovered on site; construction crew keeps the secret, but one blabs in local bar late at night.

Day 181 – Pickets from local Native American tribe appear at job site; other tradesmen, dray drivers refuse to cross picket lines.

Days 182-186 – Negotiations with local tribe; work stalled.

Day 187 – Shaman located to properly and respectfully deal with Native American remains, which are then remanded to Island burial mound.

Days 188-194 – Work resumes; first floor framing completed.

Day 195 – Summer motor vehicle rules prevent electric and telephone cables from being laid.

Day 196 – 210 – Workers' summer vacation; required by union rules.

Day 211 – 228 – Refreshed, workers have longest period of continuous work.

Day 229 – City building inspector halts work; basement joists not built according to specifications.

Days 230-245 – Basement joists taken out, building shored up, new joists delivered and installed.

Days 246-255 – Second floor framing completed.

Days 256-266 – Work halted, roof frames too big to be hauled by dray, motor vehicle permit not available until mid-October.

Days 267-270 – Work crew, idled for ten days, resumes old habits; hangovers persist for three days.

Days 271-298 – Work continues on everything but roof; first phase of plumbing installed, water hooked up.

Day 299 – Beginning of deer season; all Island men, including visiting workers, off to Bois Blanc Island for ensuing 14 days.

Day 314 – Workers return to work; most of day spent regaling co-workers with deer camp stories.

Day 317 – Unsuspecting downstate workers shocked when winter comes early; unable to reach job site on their bikes due to 2 foot snow drifts; no rental snowmobiles to be had.

Days 318-321 – Work suspended pending end of record-breaking snow fall and 6° temperatures.

Day 322 – Workers return to job site to find ground frozen, water pipes burst, half-finished building flooded and iced over.

Day 323 – Downstate crew seen catching last boat off the Island and heading south.

Day 596 – Project completed by local crew at twice original estimate.

Day 597 – Owner visits Bankruptcy Court; files for Chapter 11.

    Don't say I didn't warn you.

Cynthia and Dennis Cawthorne in a ceremonial photo behind the taps during the grand opening of the Village Inn, June 1981.

Saloon Keeper

I never in my life expected to be a saloon keeper, but Mackinac Island has a funny way of doing unexpected things to people.

During my Chamber of Commerce days and for several years after, I would periodically say to business owner acquaintances, "If you ever think about selling, give me a call." I envisioned a side investment that would allow me to ply my full-time professional interests and yet keep one foot inside the Island business community.

In the spring of 1973 I received a call from John Ross saying his Murray Hotel was for sale and it was mine for an asking price that was very low even by the standards of the day. Inexplicably, I turned him down. "I'm too busy in the Legislature right now, so it just won't work," I told him. I spent the next decade hating myself and looking for a chance at redemption.

It came in 1978 when Jack Chambers decided to divest himself of his two Main Street stores and their vacant backyard. Jack offered me the back lot at a fair price -- not too high, not too low -- and I took him up on it. Now the question was, what to do with it. After meditating on the matter in the two years following my retirement from the Legislature, I decided to seek one of the new resort liquor licenses recently made available by the State to qualifying entities. My project met the guidelines. I received Jack's permission to use the Village Inn name, lined up an architect and builder, and secured a loan from a Straits area bank, approval of which was contingent on the bank president's nephew getting the contract to supply all of our fresh white fish. We were off and running.

Only one obstacle remained, getting City Council permission to actually utilize our state-issued liquor license. In most communities this is a pro-forma, a mere formality. Not on Mackinac. One council member said he would vote "yes" only if I promised I would serve the exact same kind of steakburgers Jack Chambers served in the old VI. (I said "yes," but he never did patronize the place after it opened). Another said he would be voting "no" because he had his own liquor license and saloon and frankly didn't want the competition. (Aren't there conflict of interest laws on those sorts of things?) Still another thought there were already too many liquor outlets on the Island. (He should have waited a few years!) Another said he would be out of town and wouldn't be around for the next two Council meetings. (It was late fall and hunting season took precedence). Suddenly, securing four "yes" votes (out of six) was beginning to look like no sure thing. In the end the good guys won (just barely with four "yes" votes), and the new Village Inn opened for business June 10, 1981.

I was worldly-wise enough to know that running a restaurant was no piece of cake. On Mackinac, however, I thought the downside somewhat limited due mainly to a captive market and an annual six-month winter hiatus. I discovered even that was not enough to

Bartenders Dean Huesdash (L) and Paul Caron (R) await their first customers at the grand opening of the Village Inn, June 1981.

stem assorted disasters and crises: our head chef, Kevin, was legally blind and on one occasion served a customer a raw fish dinner; the manager had a sudden need in late season to order multiple cases of an exotic liquor, the bottles of which quickly disappeared without any corresponding increase in liquor sale revenues; we had originally installed no air-conditioning and the first summer was unusually hot; we installed air-conditioning the next

Ron and Mary Dufina, who operated the Village Inn from 1984 to 2011, take delivery from Anheuser-Busch's famous Clydesdales.

year and the summer was unusually cool; the grandmothers of countless waitstaff became "sick" in mid- and late August necessitating their return home to comfort the afflicted before our busy, often make-or-break Labor Day weekend. And so on.

 I actually enjoyed being actively involved in the restaurant and bar business but in late 1983, Cynthia and I concluded a deal to turn operations of our property over to Ron and Mary Dufina who had several other successful Island enterprises. The new operators did a good job. They expanded the Village Inn's hours and seasons, diversified its menu, and in general gave the business more attention than I was able to with a full-time law practice 220 miles downstate. After 27 years of that arrangement, in November 2011 we entered into a new relationship with owners of Grand Hotel. They assumed operations a month later and Cawthorne's Village Inn entered into a new era in affiliation with an iconic name and sterling reputation.

Canadian sailor Hilt Fraser, a popular volunteer entertainer at the Mustang Lounge from the 1970s through the 1990s. He, his son, and locals combined to produce a CD of popular Mackinac-themed ballads.

The Evolving Bar Scene

The enjoyment of beverages, particularly of the alcoholic kind, has always been a big part of Mackinac Island in all seasons. Given the boredom of winter and the carnival atmosphere of summer it would be astonishing if it were otherwise.

Toss in the thirsty and heated hormonal state of hundreds of young Island student workers away from home or school for the first time and . . . well, you get the picture. The latter factor reached a fever pitch on the Island in the summer of 1972 when, under changes to Michigan law, 18-year-olds could drink legally. Michigan legislators and state lawmakers all over the country soon saw the folly of the experiment, and within a few years under-21 drinking was just a memory on Mackinac and nearly everywhere.

I do not recall large numbers of Island workers—or even the travelling public— packing the bars at night in the 1960s. That came later with 18-year-old drinking. By the mid-1970s nearly every summer night would find the Island's "in" places jam-packed until closing time. The "in" places changed over the years, as "in" places always do. When I first came to Mackinac, Horn's Palm Café, featuring a horse-shoe shaped bar, was the favorite place of locals. Entertainment, which was rare, usually consisted of a lone piano player pounding out a tired array of "oldies." The Pink Pony, patronized mainly by packaged tour groups, rocked not at all save for the two weeks of yacht races. Its featured entertainment was an elderly piano player named Mildred Davis who doubled as organist at the Little Stone Church. (The last thing some husbands remembered on a Saturday night was the sight of Mildred banging on the Pink Pony piano and, dragged by their wives to Sunday services, the first thing they saw through bleary eyes the next morning was the same gray-haired lady belting out religious hymns on the Congregational church organ.)

The Village Inn and Mary's Pantry were small and patronized mainly by locals. Hardy's was almost exclusively the domain of the Island's black workers. The original Village Inn in 1961 added a second floor lounge with a panoramic view of Main Street and the harbor. When I reincarnated the "new" Village Inn in 1981 it became, a few years later under the Dufina management, a number-one choice of the student/worker crowd. Horn's, owned and operated by Patti Ann Moskwa, energetic grand-daughter of Amos Horn, and her husband Stephen, emerged as the Island's first choice for late night entertainment and action.

The Mustang, formerly Hardy's and under the new ownership of Dennis Brodeur, eventually supplanted Horn's as the Island's "local" bar and in winter doubled as a virtual community center. Harry Ryba, of fudge fame, opened the Pilot House in a corner of the Lake View Hotel and packed it every night until he suddenly decided to close it down in favor of a retail shop. Next door to it, many years later, Goodfellows opened and attracted Lake View Hotel patrons and a contingent of locals.

Other changes in the bar scene occurred over the years. Mary's Pantry gave way to Sandra and Debra Orr's expanded (and later much renovated) French Outpost. They in turn sold to Grand Hotel which successfully operated it as the The Gatehouse. A surge of new licensed beverage outlets ensued in the late 1990s and after. Ty's (later Huron Street Pub), Millie's on Main, Mary's Bistro, Stonecliffe, The Woods, Yankee Rebel, and Seabiscuit all made their appearance. Proof that not every hotel was enamored of the bar business came when the Murray, highly popular for its "fish bowl" tables behind large windows fronting on Main Street, quit the liquor business in the late 1970s.

On Mackinac it's not just people who patronize the bars. On at least two occasions, locals rode (or attempted to ride) their horses into the bars, and in the late 1980s a Budweiser Clydesdale managed to make it onto the dance floor of one of them. Whether the Clydesdale then performed a polka or a rhumba is unrecorded.

Steve and Patti Ann Moskwa took over Horn's Bar, formerly The Palm Cafe, from Patti Ann's grandparents, Amos and Nell Horn, in the late 1970s and turned it into a popular night spot. For many years before that, it was the Island's lone winter-time watering hole.

Fiddling around at the Mustang in mid-winter. L-R seated, Pat Squires, Bill Squires, Delia Perault, Kitty Horn. L-R standing, Sylvia Perault, Sue (Perault) Chambers, Canadian fiddler Fred LaPerrier, Dan Seeley.

There's more than one way to get to the two bar-restaurants open on the Island in winter: a bundled-up pedestrian, snowmobiles, and Bill Chambers with team and vintage sleigh on December 31, 1999.

Detroit Free Press

On Guard For 158 Years

SUNDAY
September 10, 1989
For home delivery call 222-6500
75 cents

Fire hits Mackinac Island
2 summer workers killed; 4 downtown stores destroyed

JOHN McDERMOTT/Associated Press

Fire fighters hose down a Mackinac Island storefront building after a 3 a.m. fire that destroyed four businesses and killed two people Saturday.

BY DAVID HACKER
Free Press Staff Writer

MACKINAC ISLAND — Two summer workers on Mackinac Island died in a fire Saturday morning that destroyed four stores, damaged three others and threatened to wipe out a major part of downtown fronting the Straits of Mackinac.

Mackinac Island police identified the victims as Stephen Scott Kinney, 22, of Muskegon, and Michelle Ann Krizan, 21, of Kentwood.

Fire Capt. William Smith said the two were found dead on a rear hall floor near a window on the second floor of the LaSalle Building on Main Street. The two-story wooden structure, owned by Frank Nephew and Bob Benser was built around the turn of the century. It once housed the

File photo
The scene of the Mackinac Island fire, shown in a 1977 photo.

Temple Theater, which showed silent films, and the post office and Western Union office.

The businesses destroyed were Betty's Gifts, Everybody's Little Mexico, the Leather Corral and the Birches gift shop. Badly damaged were Kilwin's Candy Shop, the Just Seasonal shop and the Big Store. The latter store was also gutted in a fire on Oct. 15, 1987, the island's last major fire.

Kathy Belanger, a police dispatcher on the island, said a woman who lives at the rooming house called about 3 a.m. to report that a couch was on fire.

Sgt. John Garcia of the State Police post in St. Ignace said authorities suspect someone smoking a cigarette may have inadvertently started the blaze.

Smith said: "the alarm sounded at 3 a.m. Our men went in and started searching the rooms but were forced out by flames. The two bodies were found in the rear hall by the windows.

See FIRE, Page 8A

2 summer workers killed in Mackinac Island blaze

FIRE, from Page 1A

It looked like they were trying to get out. The first one they found was the girl. Neither body was burned at all. They had to be overcome by smoke."

Police Chief Lawrence Jones said, "Most of the rooms were empty when the fire began as summer workers, mostly college students, had already left the island."

Nephew said the second floor contained rooms rented to as many as 30 employees during the summer season. Fewer than six employees were in the building Saturday, he said, adding: "Most of them are gone, thank God."

Bartenders at the French Outpost, a bar and dining room near the Grand Hotel, said the dead couple had been there Friday night. Several people said Krizan was a waitress at the Iroquois Hotel, and Kinney worked as a driver for Arrowhead Carriage Tours.

The fire caused the entire block on Main Street to be evacuated, and some residents living across the alley behind the burning buildings also were told to leave.

Hermann Schwaiger, a chef at the Grand Hotel who lives on Market Street behind the burned block, said: "Smoke was coming into my apartment bad. When I looked out I saw a bright spot above the buildings, but no flames were visible. Only once did I see a little bitty flame."

William Twerwilliger, who runs a curio and gift shop on Market, across the alley from the LaSalle Building, said that when he came downtown at 8:30 a.m. thick black smoke still was hanging over Main Street.

An early-morning drizzle turned into a downpour at midday, but by then it was too late to help extinguish the fire, said Smith.

Smith said the fire apparently started in the room near where the dead couple was found. He said damage would amount to "at least $1 million. I wouldn't guess beyond that."

For five hours, ferry service to the island was stopped while ferry boats brought over fire fighters and equipment, and evacuated dozens of islanders.

Seven area fire departments assisted the 22-person Mackinac Island Fire Department in fighting the fire, which was finally brought under control at 10 a.m., said Jones.

Most motorized vehicles are banned from the island, which has only about 400 year-round residents. But the island's fire department has four trucks, including one formerly owned by the Detroit suburb of Southfield and delivered Friday.

Fire

Traveling in Europe in September 1989, over morning coffee my eye caught the dateline of a story in an English language newspaper, "Mackinac Island, Michigan. —Two Students Die in Resort Island Fire," read the caption over the short, two paragraph story, and it identified Mackinac's LaSalle Building as the site of the tragedy. Six stores were also damaged or destroyed, and losses were estimated to be in the millions of dollars, the story continued.

I myself had lived in the LaSalle during my first year as Chamber of Commerce manager. Finding the nearest international telephone (at that time and place, no easy task) I called back to the United States for details. One of the victims was 22-year-old Stephen Kinney, the only son of political supporters of mine back in the days when I represented the Muskegon area in the state legislature. The other victim was his 21-year-old girl friend, Michelle Krizan, of Kentwood, Michigan. Kinney, a navy veteran and Lansing Community College student, had driven for Arrowhead Carriages and Krizan, a Michigan State University senior, worked as a waitress at the Iroquois Hotel. Both succumbed to smoke inhalation, the fire in all probability caused by a cigarette dropped in a hallway sofa around 3 a.m.

The couple, the *Detroit Free Press* said "were a campus love story, woven out of parties and a love of swimming and horses, spending their last two summers together working on Mackinac Island, enjoying each other and the tourists who make the resort tick . . . They were perfect for each other. They were very much in love." In a final irony, both young people had earlier left the Island for the season but came back for one final weekend to earn extra money. The LaSalle itself, which earlier had housed 50 workers, was scheduled to close completely for the season later on the very day of the fire.

The tragic events, while a small story in Europe, were headline news in Michigan. Suddenly, a spotlight had been shined on Island employee housing conditions, and it did not reveal a pretty sight. The LaSalle room of the young sweethearts did not even have a window, and one escape route stairwell had been boarded over. No sprinklers, alarm systems, or escape routes were in place. A state police report listed nine building and

fire code violations. Lack of City inspection records, inconsistent code enforcement, and other issues were also cited. Newspaper accounts correctly noted that the LaSalle's lack of elemental safety devices was not atypical of Island employee housing, and that overcrowding and unsanitary conditions were closer to the norm.

The public and the press were demanding answers and action. Mackinac County Prosecuting Attorney Prentiss M. Brown III, my good friend, withdrew from a criminal investigation of the tragedy, because close relatives had owned the LaSalle until it was sold to two Island businessmen three years earlier. Citing potential conflicts of interest, Brown turned the matter over to State Attorney General Frank J. Kelley who ten years later would become my partner in private law practice. The possibility of criminal charges being filed was very real, but in the end state authorities, including Kelley, threw the full weight of their efforts into getting Mackinac to fix its huge and obvious problem. Within weeks, regular fire safety inspections were made mandatory, code regulations strictly enforced. Sprinkler and alarm systems were installed in commercial buildings all over town and ways of ingress and egress carefully constructed and marked. Maximum room capacities were set and clean-up generally the order of the day. Many businesses embarked on building new and safer employee housing structures. Out of the terrible LaSalle tragedy there arose a new respect for the danger of fire and a will to make the Island safer then it had been before. As tragic as their deaths were, Stephen Kinney and Michelle Krizan did not die in vain.

There were other major and tragic fires in my half century on the Island, though none aroused the passion and grabbed the headlines more than the LaSalle fire. In July 1964, Nellie Doud, 90 years old and blind, died of smoke inhalation in a house fire just 20 feet away from the apartment in which I lived that summer. It occurred on one of the two nights of the whole summer that I was away from the Island, attending my grandmother's funeral in Manistee. In September 1967 the Ray Summerfield home near British Landing burned on the Friday night of the biennial Michigan Republican Conference which I was attending. In the aftermath, Summerfield sold his now vacant piece of lakefront property to John McCabe, Shakesperian actor and biographer of Jimmy Cagney, reserving, however, one hundred feet of lakefront between Lakeshore Boulevard and the waters of Lake Huron. It was this parcel, created in the aftermath of the house fire, that I bought from Summerfield in 1970 for the construction of my very own Island home.

In 1978, fire destroyed the West Bluff home of Mr. and Mrs. Alvin Sherman and for a time threatened Grand Hotel itself. The State Park Commission, before I was a member, agonized over what to do with the resultant vacant land, the issue being whether to allow construction of a new Victorian style cottage or to maintain the West Bluff as a preserve

of the truly original and not allow a reconstruction. The latter course prevailed, and today a large beautiful open garden separates two original West Bluff homes.

The explosion of a propane gas line serving Mission Point Resort caused a private Main Street residence to be blown to bits and its three occupants, Richard Hadden, Frances Hadden, and Sheldon Roots, old-time MRA members who remained on the Island after the MRA had pulled up stakes. The site is now a four-unit condominium.

In October 1987, just three years before the LaSalle tragedy, a major fire destroyed The Big Store, the Island's only brick commercial building. In a story titled, "The Miracle that Saved Mackinac Island," the *Detroit Free Press* said, "what saved Mackinac Island was a spectacular and unpredictable set of circumstances." One of those circumstances was that just nine months earlier, Mackinac Island had put on line a $2 million water and sewer system, with two reservoir tanks holding a million and a quarter million gallons respectively. Under the old system, the reservoir would have been pumped dry in 20 minutes.

The second circumstance was an unprecedented marshalling of fire-fighting personnel and equipment from all over the Straits area. St. Ignace sent a fire truck aboard the Mackinac Island State Park landing barge and its 14-member fire-fighting crew aboard an Arnold ferryboat. Mackinaw City dispatched a 10-person crew aboard Shepler's ferry, along with a water cannon that fired 1,500 gallons a minute over long distances. The U.S. Coast Guard sent seven crewmen from St. Ignace and two police officers each came from St. Ignace, Mackinaw City, the Michigan State Police and the Mackinac County Sheriff's Department.

Disaster by fire, on what one newspaper called "the island built to burn," had been narrowly averted.

Until at least the early 1970s, the Island's volunteer fire department was long on dedication but short on equipment and training. Pictured here, about a decade before my arrival, are front (L-R), Chief Jimmy Chapman, Ty Horn, Fred Schmidt (driver), Junior Davenport, Wilson LaPine, and Jerry Wessel. Back (L-R), John Bloswick and Dick LaPine. Today's 28 Island volunteers are well-trained and their equipment state-of-the-art.

Members of the 1973 volunteer fire department stand in front of their new (and only) truck: L-R, Chief Armand "Smi" Horn, Robert "Porky" LaPine, Bill Squires, George Wellington, Bill Smith, and Elmer "Bud" Bradley. In the 1950s and 1960s both the State Park and Moral Re-Armament maintained their own one-truck volunteer fire department.

2013 Mackinac Island firefighters, several members of a much larger police force, and curious on-lookers in front of the historic Community Hall. Chief Mike Bradley and Assistant Chief Jason St. Onge at left.

Even the youngest and littlest get in on the Island's fundraiser mania. The Chamber of Commerce manager gives an assist in 1962 to three-year-old Sandy Ecker collecting contributions for the medical center on "Daisy Day."

The Taxes Ain't Bad, It's the Fundraisers That Kill Ya'

For many years the Mackinac Island city assessor deliberately kept property valuations low. In the 1980s neighboring Mackinac county units of government complained, correctly pointing out that comparatively low Island assessments necessitated higher county millages to make up the artificial shortfall. In the summer of 1991 the *Detroit Free Press* leaped on the story and related the example of one West Bluff home being assessed at a market value of $266,000 while being offered for sale at $2 million. Said the paper, "Some (Island) properties are valued for tax purposes like they were part of the idyllic, suspended-in-time myth that permeates the Island."

By 1993 an unwelcome Island-wide reassessment was finally undertaken. Property owners saw their valuations – and their taxes – double and even triple. All of this bad news, however, was moderated by the fact that the Island had (and has) one of the lowest millage rates in the state. In 2013 that total millage rate was 21.7 for homesteads and 29.5 for commercial property and second homes.

Those comparatively low local property taxes are the good news. But Mackinac Islanders are regularly tapped above and beyond mere taxes. Fundraising events of every kind and for every cause abound on the Island. Raffle tickets sometimes seem like the hottest commodity in town. And woe to the reputation of one who refuses to buy. Every year a minimum of a dozen, often as many as twenty, causes pursue their quarry, raking in dollars and goods for the medical center, arts council, horsemen's association, state park, school, chamber of commerce, hospitals, community foundation, scholarships, churches, and political war chests. The Island response is invariably generous and there is an unspoken acknowledgment that virtually all of the causes are worthy and contributions to them a civic duty.

Monetary contributions are not the whole story, however. Locals and cottagers from every walk of life contribute their own unique skills and talents to an array of causes: Harrisonville's Caroline LaPine and Don Andress hand-crafting their wares to be auctioned off at the annual Christmas Bazaar; the late Stella King and the late Evangeline ("Ling") Horn from the Mission area donating hours of time initiating the first Lilac Day over sixty years ago; Lorna Straus and Kay Hoppenrath leading a myriad of community causes; Harrisonville's Armand "Smi" Horn, volunteer fireman and city council member for nearly a half century; hotel proprietor Vic Callewaert, indefatigable raffle ticket seller; the West Bluff's Richard and Jane Manoogian, community benefactors on a grand scale; teacher Dan Seely, nurse Ed Chambers, and business owner Tim Leeper, chefs at innumerable community suppers; the Timmons and Rearick families, quietly and generously supporting a myriad of undertakings; the East Bluff's Tom and Kathy Lewand, providing leadership to numerous community endeavors; Paul Wandrie, champion of veterans' causes; Mike Carley and David Levy, one a local gardener the other a wealthy summer cottager, auctioneers at countless fundraisers; Steve Rilenge, Leanne Brodeur, and Becki Barnwell, kick-starting new civic endeavors against great odds; and cottagers Mike and Wendy Young, helpful in many endeavors, to name just some because of the impossibility or impracticality of naming all.

It can safely be said that a substantial number of local property owners shell out more in local charitable contributions than they do in property taxes. As one tapped-out summer cottager described it to me many years ago, "On Mackinac the taxes ain't bad . . . it's the fundraisers that kill ya'."

Richard and Jane Manoogian, generous contributors to numerous Island fundraisers. Their gift made possible a new State Park-operated art museum in the renovated Indian Dormitory that served as the Island's K-10 school when I first came to the Island.

Locals and visitors fill the Island's Community Hall for the Christmas Bazaar held each year the first weekend in December. The event benefits an array of local charities.

A Taxing Situation

The comparatively low property taxes Mackinac Islanders enjoy were nearly wiped out and replaced with a mammoth tax hike in 1994, one whose impact – had it happened – would be felt to this day. That I was able to prevent it, with some timely help, is one of the very best things I ever accomplished for the Island, at least if measured in dollars and cents.

Until 1994 Michigan financed its K-12 schools with a system that relied heavily on local property taxes that varied greatly from one school district to another. Districts with comparatively low property values needed rates of 37 mills and upward for operations and then were just barely able to keep their heads above water. In contrast, some districts with very high property values and comparatively few students were getting along very well on a low millage rate. Clearly, the system needed reform if there was to be equitable and adequate funding statewide.

In late 1993 Governor Engler engineered the total abolition of the old system and forced the Legislation to devise an alternative. It became clear to me that Mackinac Island's taxpayers would be huge losers in any reform effort. This was because Mackinac's very high property values per pupil meant that few mills were needed to support its school of less than 100 students. In fact, under the existing system, Mackinac school had the second lowest millage rate in the state (approximately 7.8) while having the second highest per pupil revenue (approximately $10, 000). A leveling of property tax wealth and millage rates, as fair as it was for the State as a whole, was sure to be a disaster for Mackinac.

As debate on a new system got underway I learned that legislative leaders, meeting behind closed doors, were close to an agreement. Under the proposed plan school operating taxes on non-homesteads (i.e. commercial property and second homes) would in most cases be capped at 18 mills plus an additional 6 mills that would be levied on all real property. For most Michigan commercial property and second home owners this was great news: their school operating taxes would fall from as much as 35 or 40 mills to just 24 mills. For Mackinac Island's owners of commercial property and second homes, the proposal would be an unmitigated disaster. Their property taxes for school operations would more than triple, going from 7.8 mills to 24.

The commercial and second-home owners of one other school district faced similar calamitous numbers. That was Bridgman, a small district in southwest Michigan that derived its huge property values from the presence of a nuclear power plant. Bridgman also happened to be in the State Senate district of Harry Gast, the very powerful chairman of the Senate Appropriations Committee. I had served with Gast when he was a member of the House Republican caucus of which I was leader. Pulling Gast out of the negotiations, I explained to him the ramifications of the proposed plan for Bridgman and Mackinac and the need for a tweak that would fix our mutual problem without upsetting the rest of the complex plan.

With the help of the Engler Administration, Gast and I put together a "fix." While the six mills on all real property would be retained, the mills levied on non-homesteads would be reduced to 18 mills or the number of mills currently being levied, whichever was less. The practical effect for Mackinac was that the levy on non-homesteads (commercial and second homes) would only go to 13.8 mills instead of the 24 mills that would have been the amount had we not intervened with our "fix."

In 2012 alone, because of our work, Mackinac Island commercial and second-home property owners saved $1.7 million, a remarkable number for one small island. Over the 18 years since our "fix," Mackinac taxpayers have been saved somewhere between $15 and $20 million dollars in property taxes. I like to think that by that one 1994 action, even if I never did another good deed for the Island, I would have earned a good, long rest.

The 1994 change in Michigan school finance, however, did have some negative consequences for the Island school. Enrollment began to slowly fall and since the new system of school aid was based in part on pupil headcount, the Island began to feel the squeeze. Consequently, in the late 1990s I prodded the Legislature to provide some special funding to island schools like Beaver and Mackinac which were "isolated" and where consolidation was impractical. I was successful and pleased that Kitty McNamara, Beaver Island Superintendent of Schools, and Gary Urman, the Mackinac Superintendent, went out of their way to show their appreciation.

Later, Sen. Jason Allen, representing both islands, took our early efforts one step further and created an on-going "isolated districts" line item in the state school-aid budget. Over the years my efforts and those of Sen. Allen have resulted in thousands of additional badly-needed dollars to Mackinac Island's school, all of it against a backdrop of savings its taxpayers millions of dollars.

On another occasion I was also able to save Islanders a substantial amount of money. Long after it had ceased the practice elsewhere, AT&T continued to impose long-distance charges on calls between the Island and its nearest mainland communities. I fought the company on that issue before the Michigan Public Service Commission and in early 2002 forced AT&T to provide no-toll service between the Island and St. Ignace, a savings of thousands of dollars collectively for Island phone customers.

The Michigan summer Governor's summer residence, deeded to the State Park Commission in 1945, sits atop a bluff with commanding views of the Straits of Mackinac.

Governor's Residence

Over a quarter century before Michigan provided an executive residence for its governor in Lansing, the capital city, it acquired one on Mackinac Island. Variously described as a mansion, cottage, or residence, the Governor's summer home on Mackinac has always been an iconic source of pride for Michigan's citizens.

The Mackinac residence, purchased for its original 1902 construction cost, has been a political gathering place—and political football—since the State Park Commission first acquired it in 1944. Described as "the best political perk of any governor in the United States," the home high on Mackinac's bluffs features 24 rooms of Georgia yellow pine and Michigan white pine, including 11 bedrooms and 9 bathrooms. A spectacular view of the Straits of Mackinac, both peninsulas, and the Mackinac Bridge is perhaps its greatest feature. Until a thorough but historically correct refurbishment and re-furnishing in the early 1990s, however, it was in its interior decidedly not the opulent place many imagined.

Mackinac had been a favorite vacation spot for the state's governors going back to the early twentieth century. In 1935 and 1936 Gov. Frank D. Fitzgerald commandeered one of the two state park cottages next to Fort Mackinac and used it for an informal summer residence. When Michigan was selected to host the 1945 National Governors Conference, the Park Commission, Bill Doyle in the forefront, pursued acquisition of the Lawrence Young cottage which had been built in 1902 for the then munificent—but by 1944 paltry—sum of $15,000. The wily Doyle made sure that the legislative act specified that the deed to the property be in the name of the Commission. That made the Commission the Governor's landlord but since its members are chosen by him (or her) it usually knew enough to treat its tenant very gingerly in matters affecting the residence.

The first governor to occupy the residence was Harry F. Kelly whose large family found it very much to their liking, despite some of the austere furnishings which included surplus army cots. In the summer of 1946 Kelly used the home to entertain, among others, Esther Williams and Jimmy Durante, the stars of MGM's *This Time for Keeps* which was filmed that year on the Island. When G. Mennen Williams' family moved in during the

Harry F. Kelly, the first governor to occupy the state's newly-acquired summer residence embraces movie stars Esther Williams and Jimmy Durante on Mackinac while Mrs. Kelly looks on. *This Time for Keeps* was filmed on the island in winter and in the summer of 1946. One of Kelly's five children, Brian, went on to be a Hollywood star in his own right as the lead in of the television series *Flipper*.

summer of 1949 they were appalled by some of the furnishings and sought a legislative appropriation to cure the matter. The legislature, inspired by Doyle's antipathy for Williams, balked, then eventually partially relented.

Use of the residence each summer, complete with a chef and housekeeper, has reflected each governor's personal preference. The Williams family loved it, and Mackinac became their second home during much of that governor's twelve year tenure. His successor, John Swainson, also used it liberally. George Romney's family visited less, but the governor did use it for strategizing with members of his administration and wooing key legislators. When Bill Milliken succeeded to the governorship in 1969, he originally used the residence minimally. A very private man, Milliken, unlike some of his predecessors, did not use Mackinac for courting legislators or many other public purposes. Although I was his party's leader in the House and was in essence his neighbor on the Island, at no time was I or (to the best of my knowledge) any other legislator ever invited to join Milliken at the residence. As time passed Milliken, like so many others, developed an affinity for the Island and by the time his 14-year occupation of the governorship came to an end in 1983 he searched for an Island home of his own. G. Mennen Williams also acquired a home on the Island in 1961 after he left the governorship.

By contrast, Gov. Jim Blanchard reveled in entertaining at his Island residence and capped it off by taking his wedding vows (for the second time) there in the summer of 1990. The Englers also made extensive use of the residence, and I was a guest of theirs at numerous public and private affairs.

In early 1991 the residence got its first badly needed renovation, just in time for John Engler's first trip to the Island as governor. The two-phase project cost nearly $1 million and was funded through a combination of public and private monies. Then, just four years later, a second renovation commenced costing over another million dollars in fix-ups and new furnishings. This time, inspectors found porches and foundations so rotted they were in danger of imminent collapse. In 2013 still another overhaul took place, this one costing $700,000.

No home renovation ever goes smoothly when the varying tastes of two spouses are involved. The Mackinac project was no exception. Attorney General Frank Kelley had given Gov. Jim Blanchard a moosehead for the mansion in the 1980s. Its unceremonious history included hanging in a Detroit bar that had gone belly-up. Engler loved the inherited moosehead. Mrs. Engler, a favorite with State Park personnel, did not. A deal was struck. Said the governor, "If you let me keep the moose, I'll stay out of the renovation." He kept his word, she kept hers. At last report, the moosehead was still mounted in the mansion.

Virtually every Governor and First Lady have enjoyed the Residence and acted as gracious hosts when the public came to call. One occupant of the Residence during my time was not among that number, however. This gubernatorial wife demanded that an elderly local summer resident be barred from ever entering the Residence after the woman, while serving as a docent, was overheard saying something that didn't meet the First Lady's approval. On another occasion, the same spouse raged at staff when she showed up at the Residence to find that a fire had not been built in the fireplace in advance of her arrival as she had instructed. When, on another occasion, State Park staff correctly and courageously told the First Lady that changes she wanted to the Governor's Residence could not proceed because they would compromise the building's historical integrity, she spent the next year awaiting her opportunity for revenge for that and other perceived grievances.

Over the years, Presidents John F. Kennedy, Harry S. Truman, George H.W. Bush, and Bill Clinton have been guests at the residence. President Gerald Ford slept overnight in 1975. He was not the only non-family member to savor an overnight there, as I learned in overhearing a conversation one evening in a downtown bar. A young man, who I knew to be on the Governor's Residence staff, was regaling a friend about his various exploits. The talk turned to women. Wouldn't his boss, the Governor, be surprised, he said, if she only knew

that while she was attending to affairs of state down in Lansing, he was having the sexual romp of his life "right there in the Governor's bed." (Word tends to get around in a small town.)

Inevitably this prize perk of the Michigan governor has been at times a political football, the target of publicity-seeking opponents of whoever the incumbent occupant might be. Sell the mansion and save taxpayer dollars, goes the refrain. A fairly recent, but certainly not the first, assault came in 2003. The Republican leader of the Senate and the chair of the House Appropriations committee jointly called on Gov. Granholm to consider selling the residence "as a luxury the state can no longer afford." They estimated the state's deficit could thereby be cut by $1.5 million Again in 2010, a major candidate for governor in that year's state election told members of the Greater Detroit Chamber of Commerce assembled at Grand Hotel that he, too, favored selling the residence.

As Commission chair, I had a terse response. As reported in the *Detroit Free Press*, I said, "The cost to maintain the house is pretty small. The prestige it gives us is pretty big. The idea of selling it is pretty stupid."

Despite the sporadic desire of some politicians to sell the residence, is it even possible or feasible to do so? The answer, I believe, is no. If the land on which the cottage rests is sold, it would trigger the reversion clause that the federal government inserted in its deed to the state back in 1895 that says "if the State ceases to use the land for the purpose aforesaid (a state park) it shall revert to the United States."

What about the residence itself being sold as personal property without the land? The Commission itself answered that in a June 2009 public memorandum: "Only the Commission has the authority to sell the building. Even if it were to do so, the proceeds from such a sale would stay with the Commission. However, the Commission is not in the business of selling its historic treasures. Such an action would be contrary to the Commission's stewardship responsibilities. It would be a direct violation of its public trust and mission to "protect, preserve, and present Mackinac's rich historic and natural resources." The Commission, therefore, has no intention of selling this structure or any of its historic buildings, collections, or other resources for a short term financial gain."

Former First Lady Anne Kelly came back to the residence in 1985 as a guest of Gov. and Mrs. James Blanchard.

Governor and Mrs. John Engler welcome Dennis and Cynthia Cawthorne to the first Engler-era summer garden party sponsored by Friends of Mackinac, 1991. The "traditional" event began in 1983 and would run for twenty years until its "perhaps timely" demise in 2003.

A Mackinac Summer Tradition

On January 1, 1983, after nearly fourteen years under William G. Milliken, Michigan had a new governor. James J. Blanchard had been largely unknown outside of the Oakland County district he represented in the U.S. Congress prior to his ascent to the state's top office. He would soon be our neighbor, the newest occupant of the Mackinac Island Governor's Residence, but virtually no one—including me—had even met him. Not good, especially for one—like me—in the business of shaping and molding state affairs and decision-making. Not good, also, for Mackinac Island's need to capture, through persuasion and friendly relations, a share of the State's largesse in the form of increased appropriations for its school, state park, and a myriad of other local needs.

I had an idea. Perhaps Friends of Mackinac, the informal group that annually hosted Lansing receptions, could host and pay for a "Welcome to Mackinac" party for the new Governor and his wife. It would be a true community event and I would put together a comprehensive invitation list of Island residents ranging from business owners to street sweepers, from Main Street to Harrisonville. In all, over 200 invitations went out and I was proud of the fact that we had covered every strata of local society. I solemnly explained to the new Governor's staff that there existed an Island tradition: the community hosts the Governor every summer after an election and in the intervening non-election years the Governor hosts the community. In truth, I had just created the "tradition." I hoped God would forgive me, at least this one time, on the grounds that this was actually a good thing for all parties involved.

Governor Blanchard graciously agreed to the arrangement and I reserved a large reception area at Mission Point Resort (the newest incarnation of the old Moral Re-Armament property) for the Sunday of Memorial Day weekend 1983. The appointed day dawned gray, cold, and ominous. Two hours before the scheduled 5 p.m. start, the heavens opened in a raw, wet deluge that was interspersed with large white snowflakes uncommon in late May. Electric lights flickered all over town, then went out. Island telephones inexplicably quit working. At Mission Point, the staff went into panic mode as the hour arrived and the hors d' oeuvres turned cold. Guests, including the Governor, groped about in a semi-darkness relieved only by faint candlelight. Fortunately, the bar continued to function, enough to guarantee success for any Mackinac social event, and the party went on despite Mother Nature's best (or worst) efforts. When it was over, all agreed that the party for the Governor had proven to be a smashing success. The "tradition" was off to an auspicious beginning.

Keeping his end of the bargain, Blanchard in 1984, 1985, and 1986 hosted community cocktail parties at the Governor's Residence and locals enthused that this was indeed a wonderful local tradition. In 1987, following Blanchard's 1986 re-election, it was again Friends of Mackinac's turn to host the party and we dutifully met our obligation. Blanchard reciprocated at the Residence in 1988, 1989, and 1990.

With the coming of John Engler to the governorship in 1991 the parties, if anything, got bigger and better. Islanders brought along their friends, a few house guests even planning their entire vacations around the annual event. The wine flowed liberally, the hors d' oeuvres were plentiful as Islanders and friends rubbed elbows with the Chief Executive and First Lady on the lawn and porches of the Residence. (By now, regardless of whose turn it was to host, the Residence had become the exclusive site of the annual event.) On one memorable occasion, a neatly attired summer resident, imbibing too long at the cocktail station, rolled in coat and tie fifteen feet down one of the Residence's grassy, manicured embankments, giggling all the way.

It became gradually apparent that these parties, at least in the post-election years that Friends of Mackinac footed the bill, were becoming rather expensive affairs. In the early summer of 2002, therefore, after consultation with other leaders of Friends of Mackinac, it was decided to have back-to-back annual parties both to be hosted by Friends, the first to be a farewell to the Englers. The second, to be held in 2003, would welcome the new governor who would be elected in November 2002. The parties, and a gift to the Englers, would be paid for by asking (though not necessarily requiring) attendees to make a contribution to the event (the request was for $50 per attendee, as I recall, and covered both years.) In view of the increasing number of guests and the resultant significant cost, it seemed to us only fair that the parties' expenses should be shared by more than just the 30 or 40 members of Friends of Mackinac.

At least one prominent person in the community apparently thought otherwise, and it was a person who saw the Governor at least once a week when he was in town and had his

ear. Sincere and well-intentioned, but in this instance wrong in my opinion, he planted in the Governor's mind that Islanders were feeling put upon by having to share in the cost of the party and resentful of Island business people who were trying to so burden them. He was, he implied, speaking for the community and doing the Governor a great favor by blowing the whistle on this outrage of extorting $50 from every invitee. To his thinking, at least, there was indeed such a thing as a free lunch.

Controversy of this kind no Governor wants, especially when it involves a comparatively piddling social event. It was therefore no surprise that when it came time to set a date for the 2002 party, Governor Engler suddenly found his calendar filled for the rest of the summer. I couldn't blame him. With considerable embarrassment, Friends of Mackinac returned checks to the many Islanders who had stepped up to the plate to support the two events. Later in the fall, a small cake and ice-cream farewell reception for the Governor was held in a church basement. Friends of Mackinac was not asked to play a part.

The following spring, after the election of Jennifer Granholm as governor, Friends of Mackinac hosted at the Residence a watered-down version of the old party. The gift purchased for the old Governor, but never delivered, was given to the new. It was the last community wide party ever held at the Governor's Residence.

It was probably time to conclude the "tradition" anyway. The old close-knit, small-town community that existed in 1983 when the "Welcome to Mackinac" parties first began was a thing of the past. Since then, new residential neighborhoods had sprung up at Stonecliffe, Stone Brook, Sunset Forest, and Trillium Heights. Many, certainly not all, of their residents were strangers to the rest of the community, and some on both sides preferred it that way. The original concept that hometown Mackinac folks were welcoming the Governor to their little community had also been diluted by the small armies of out-of-town house guests and other hangers-on who joined the "free" party. And, finally, the financial burden of the parties on both the Governor and the forty or so supporters of Friends of Mackinac had become unsustainable. And so the music stopped.

Now, when people ask me why we don't have community parties at the Governor's like we used to "in the good old days," I give a knowing smile, and silently recall all the good times we had during the 20-year life of the "tradition" I created.

A 1963 meeting of a Commission whose members were noted for their longevity of service. Clockwise beginning at the far right W. Stewart Woodfill (12 years), Wilfird F. Doyle (40 years), Neil Downing (5 years), Park Superintendent Carl Nordberg, James Dunnigan (32 years), Walter J. Murray (25 years), Mariana (Nan) Rudolph (16 years), Historic Projects Director Eugene Petersen, and Joseph Thompson (26 years).

The State Park Commission

In 1895 the United States government transferred Mackinac National Park—the nation's second national park—and Fort Mackinac along with its military reservation on Mackinac Island to the State of Michigan.

To manage Michigan's first state park and its local land area the state legislature created and Governor John T. Rich appointed the five-member Mackinac Island State Park Commission. Thus there was set upon this single small island two governments, one being local and one being state, each independent of the other yet inextricably linked by their common issues and their common constituency.

Since 1895 the lands under the Commission's sole jurisdiction have more than doubled and now also include the mainland sites of colonial Michilimackinac in Mackinaw City and historic Mill Creek four miles to the southeast. Its jurisdiction on Mackinac Island has expanded to comprise 83% of the island's land area.[1] Also vastly expanded have been the commission's duties and responsibilities, especially since 1958.

Membership on the commission has historically been the most sought after appointment in state government. Appointees have usually been politically powerful individuals, often persons close to the Governor and nearly always persons with clout of their own or through their association with politically powerful entities. State law requires that the Commission be bi-partisan. That has given the Commission an on-going pipeline to key decision-makers in both political parties, especially important in a state like Michigan where partisan control of the legislature and governorship has tended to swing back and forth with great frequency.

Over the years, Commission members have included one former U.S. Senator (Ferry), one former U.S. Representative (Traxler), one former Secretary of State (Haggerty), one former Attorney General (Kelley), one Governor's son (Ferris), a U.S. Representative's wife (Stupak), four party national committee members (Price, Holden, Yob, and Goodman), and six state legislative leaders (White, Doyle, Hinkley, Sink, Stahlin, Cawthorne). Other

---

1   The Commission's history up to the time I became a member has been well told by the late David Armour in his book, *One Hundred Years at Mackinac*.

commissioners have been influential business leaders or distinguished in the law or other professions.

The first chairman of the five-member body was Thomas Ferry, born on the Island to missionary parents and himself a former U.S. Senator from Michigan. As President Pro Tem of the Senate, he was arguably President of the United States for a single day on March 4, 1877, when President-Elect Rutherford Hayes and his vice-president refused to be sworn in on the Sabbath, leaving Ferry next in the presidential line of succession. The man who was the second chairman was notable in his own right: Peter White of Marquette was a civic leader and philanthropist who once walked from his home in the Upper Peninsula to the state capitol in Lansing.

In 1927 the Legislature changed the 1895 law to provide that Commissioners serve at the pleasure of the Governor rather than having fixed terms. The inevitable result was a revolving door of commissioners from 1927 through all of the 1930s under Michigan's seven governors who at that time served two-year terms. The Commission slate was wiped clean in 1931, 1933, 1935, 1937, and 1939 when Republicans and Democrats alternated in holding the governorship. In the darkest days of the Depression, Commission chairman Roger Andrews also filled the position of Director and personally handled all day-to-day park operations.[2]

In 1941 the statute was changed back to fixed terms, and Bill Doyle got his "resident commission" slot which added a sixth member to the Commission. He provided additional political insulation for himself by adding a provision that no more than four Commission members could be from the same political party. Thus, when Democrats took the Governorship, Doyle still had a fighting chance to be retained which he was—with an aforementioned one short interruption in 1947—until he finally pushed G. Mennen Williams over the edge in 1955. When Fort Michillimackinac was restored in 1959 a seventh Commission seat was added and designated for a Mackinac City resident, the first appointee being Neil Downing.

During my early years on the Island, the Commission members were noted for their longevity of tenure. Joseph Thompson, first appointed in 1935, served 26 years at various times in a period lasting until 1977, the resourceful Bill Doyle 41 years between 1939 and 1985, Ken Teysen 33 consecutive years from 1964 to 1997, East Bluffer James P. Dunnigan 32 consectutive years from 1949 to 1981, and Walter J. Murray 25 consecutive years from 1959 to 1984. Mariana Rudolph in 1957 and Margaret Price in 1959, both appointed by Gov. G. Mennen Williams, were the Commission's first females. Kathleen Lewand, appointed by Gov. James Blanchard, was the first female to serve as chair and did so from 1985 until I succeeded her in 1991.

---

2   Robert Doud also held the position of Commissioner and Director, though unlike Andrews, not simultaneously. He served on the Commission in 1938 and as Park Superintendent during the World War II years of 1941-45.

In 1958, just before my arrival on the Island, the Commission's responsibilities were greatly expanded. Seeing the success of revenue bonds used to finance construction of the Mackinac Bridge, Gov. Williams envisioned revenue bonds being used to totally refurbish Fort Mackinac and turn it into an active historical museum and driver of economic growth in the Straits region. His first move was to convince W. Stewart Woodfill, owner of Grand Hotel, to accept appointment to the Commission which Woodfill did on condition that he also become its chairman. Woodfill, a staunch Republican, and Williams, prototype of the Democratic Party's most liberal wing, had earlier worked together with Prentiss Brown to gain legislative approval for construction of the Mackinac Bridge.

Both Woodfill and Williams recognized the possibility inherent in this more modest, yet economically important Fort project. Whereas then-existing state law only gave the Commission authority to maintain and operate the State Park and its slowly crumbling facilities, the new legislative act gave the Commission broad authority to "acquire, construct, develop, improve, better, extend, repair, maintain, use and operate . . . facilities of all kinds that in the judgment of the Commission will increase the beauty and utility of the state park facilities and provide recreational, historical, or other facilities for the benefit and enjoyment of the public . . . (and) to engage consulting architects, engineers, museum technicians, landscape architects, supervisors, managers, lawyers, fiscal agents, and other agents and employees as it considers necessary, and to establish their compensation . . . (and) to change admissions and other fees and rentals . . . (and) issue revenue bonds for (such) purposes."

The net result was that in 1958 the Commission went from passively watching over a park to taking on a whole new array of historical preservation and other tasks. Moreover, the Commission's powers were relatively independent of other state agencies which assured for it a vigorous, proactive role and agenda.

About the time I arrived on the Island, however, the Commission faced a threat to its independence that would require a bold and innovative response. Fortunately, the politically astute Bill Doyle was still actively representing clients before the state legislature just as effectively as ever. Having just been restored to the Commission by Governor John Swainson, Doyle convinced the 1965 Legislature, implementing decisions of Michigan's Constitutional Convention of 1961-62, to make an exception to the required consolidation of all state boards, commissions, bureaus, and agencies into twenty state departments.

Thus was created something called a "Type One" agency, a status conferred on the Mackinac Island State Park Commission and only a very small handful of other select state agencies. As a Type One agency, the MISPC was technically within the Department of Natural Resources but, very importantly, it retained its previously granted statutory authority

and responsibility for developing and implementing its own programs and projects. Whereas most other state boards and commissions have only an "advisory" role, the Mackinac Commission is autonomous, almost a separate department of state government. In coming years, the MISPC would be re-assigned (in 2001) to the Department of History, Arts, and Libraries, (in 2009) to the Department of Natural Resources and the Environment, and (in 2010) to the Department of Natural Resources. Through it all, however, it retained its very valuable Type One status, the importance of which I came to recognize and greatly appreciate when I in 1991 became a member of the Commission.

These days on the Island the Commission owns and leases out Island House hotel, owns and operates the airport, cares for all historic buildings within Fort Mackinac and eleven historic buildings outside the fort including the Governor's summer residence, supervises and regulates privately owned residences on state-leased land, maintains over 70 miles of road and trails, licenses and regulates taxis and sight-seeing carriages, grants electric, telephone, and cable TV franchises, and leases lands for golf courses, an equestrian center, youth recreation, and Island infrastructure. In its administrative and research offices on the Island and Mackinaw City, Commission staff researches and archives 80,000 books and documents in addition to over a million artifacts. Also important is the Commission's educational outreach programs and its extensive publications and tourism promotion program. Without any doubt, the Commission's role has greatly expanded since 1958.

Occasionally, there have been calls for abolishing the State Park Commission or at least its Type One status. One of those times was during the early 1990s when controversy developed over use of the Captain's and Major's Quarters. These structures, located just outside the walls of Fort Mackinac, were built in 1876, and since state takeover of the federal lands they have been used to house state officials present on the Island for official business. Like the Governor's residence, the Captain's and Major's cannot be sold without triggering the reversion clause in the 1895 deed from the United States to the State of Michigan.

When Tom Washington, head of the Michigan United Conservation Clubs and an implacable foe of the Commission, took up the cry in late 1991, I told the *Lansing State Journal*, that Washington's "real agenda is to turn over control of Michigan's premier state park to faceless bureaucrats." Commented George Weeks of the *Detroit News,* "There are, in effect, dual governments on the island. It is good for the city to have a working relationship with a commission that is not merely advisory and has to take orders from Lansing. Keeper of Michigan's historical jewel is the Mackinac Island State Park Commission. The commission should keep its special powers to protect a special place."

Indeed, in my view nothing could be worse for the Island community than abolition of the Park Commission or loss of its Type One status. Its members know, and in many cases live (at least part-time) on the island they help govern. They are accessible, are responsive, and understand the unique problems of the community in a way no Lansing-based bureaucrat could ever appreciate. Without the Commission, local impact on governance of 83% of the island would be next to nothing. Fortunately, the proposals to abolish the Commission or its Type One status have never yet gotten any serious traction and it is my hope that, long after I'm gone, they never do.

Commissioners past and present gathered at this 100 year commemoration of the Commission's first meeting on July 4, 1895. Seated L-R: Stephen Vogel, Kenneth Teysen, L. Margaret (Meg) Brown, Chuck Yob, Dennis Cawthorne, Richard Kughn, Mark Schlussel, Frank Kelley. Standing L-R: Retired Director Eugene Petersen, Deputy Director David Armour, Nino Green, Mariana (Nan) Rudolph, Michael Hegarty, Kathy Lewand, Alan Sawyer, Sheldon Smith, Eugene Curtis, James Dunnigan, Director Carl Nold.

State Park Commissioners pose on the grounds of Fort Mackinac, summer 2002. L-R, Frank J. Kelley, Richard Manoogian, Joan Porteous, Stephen Vogel, Dennis Cawthorne, Audrey Jaggi, Mark Schlussel.

COMMISSIONER

My appointment to the Mackinac Island State Park Commission by the Governor came to me as a surprise, though in retrospect I suppose it should not have. I had supported my old House colleague John Engler in his 1990 campaign for the office, but like most political observers believed his chances of winning over incumbent Jim Blanchard were between slim and none.

Shortly after Engler's surprise razor-thin upset, I happened to be in the governor-elect's transition office in Lansing. Entering the room Engler—talking loudly enough for everyone to hear but to no one in particular—pointed to me and said, "Well, there's the new Mackinac Island State Park Commissioner!" As improbable as it seems it had not even occurred to me that there was a vacancy, and I had not even contemplated the possibility of being named to it.

In fact, there really should not have been a vacancy. What happened was that Gov. Blanchard, falling far behind in filling vacancies on state commissions and boards, got into the habit of merely letting his appointees stay on when their terms expired until he got around to appointing them officially to a new term. This all worked very well until the November 1990 election. Though Blanchard's own term and his power to appoint would continue until January 1, 1991, the State Senate was Republican controlled. Since most appointments (and re-appointments) needed Senate confirmation, Blanchard was effectively cut off at the pass. Dozens of Blanchard appointees thus were subject to replacement in the middle of what would have been their new terms, and Mackinac Island Commissioner (and chair) Kathy Lewand fell into that category. Thus, on January 12, 1991, I was one of the first persons named to an appointed position in the Engler Administration, filling the balance—4 years and 3 months—of what would have been Ms. Lewand's second term.

Appointment to the Mackinac Island Commission had always been considered a major political plum. No single gubernatorial appointment has been more coveted in every Administration than a seat on the Commission. Part of the allure, it seemed, was the popularity, mystique, prestige, and perceived glamour of being associated with Mackinac

Island and its governance. Part was the perquisites of the office, real and perceived. Historically, being a Commissioner meant celebrity status on the local social scene, a team of horses and a chauffeured state carriage at a Commissioner's beck and call, use of one of the Commission's two stately Victorian cottages perched high on the cliffs overlooking the harbor, and political cache in Lansing and elsewhere. By 1991, the time of my appointment, the state carriage had fallen to the budget-cutting ax, I had my own Island home with no need for a second Island home, and I was already well-established in the Lansing political community. Nevertheless, I looked forward enthusiastically to my new position and the opportunity to do good things for Mackinac Island. A month after my appointment, on February 28, 1991, I became the Commission chair.

Finding it necessary to appoint two Democrats to the Commission because of the law's bi-partisan requirement, Gov. John Engler came to me with an unusual request shortly after I became Commission chair in 1991. "The law says I need to appoint two Democrats," he said, "and I don't know any good Democrats. Who would you suggest?" (Engler was a staunch partisan, and I was never sure whether he was totally serious in his comment or not.) Thus I was given the opportunity, for the first and only time, to in effect choose two appointees to the Commission. Engler accepted my recommendations of L. Margaret (Meg) Brown of Petoskey and Stephen Vogel of Detroit, and they were appointed in April 1991.

I did not really know Meg Brown but was very aware of her sterling record of community service in Petoskey as school board president and chair of the Emmet County Airport Board. It helped that I was well-acquainted with her various in-laws and relatives in Prentiss M. Brown's extended family, including former Commissioner Marianna (Nan) Rudolph. Steve Vogel I knew well through his leadership in American Institute of Architects Michigan Chapter, a client of our law firm. Steve was a "soft" Democrat but certainly met the bi-partisan requirement and brought valuable historic architecture experience to the Commission. Vogel was re-appointed to a second term by Engler in 1997 but he chose not to re-appoint Brown and instead asked her to join the Lake Superior State University Board.

Engler, in my opinion, was not only a very good Governor but he was also a very shrewd politician who calculated carefully in later selecting two other Democrats to serve on the Commission. Frank Kelley, as Attorney General, had already figured prominently in Commission affairs on a number of occasions. He also had an affinity for the Island based in part on his experience as a very young man working as a deckhand on the ferries plying the Straits of Mackinac between St. Ignace and Mackinaw City. In 1998 Engler was preparing to seek a third and final term as Governor and he very much wanted to also elect a Republican Attorney General. With Kelley ensconced in that office for the past 37 years his prospects, if

Kelley sought re-election, were dim. At 74 years of age, however, Kelley was plainly ready to at least contemplate the thought of not running again. Sensing this, and hoping it might tip his decision, Engler sent him an emissary bearing the message that should Kelley decide he might like to retire, a position on the Mackinac Island State Park Commission would be his for the asking. Shortly thereafter, the venerable Attorney General announced he would not seek an eleventh term. In January 1999, just days after his retirement from the Attorney Generalship, Kelley's appointment to the Mackinac Commission was made official.

The 1998 race for State Attorney General had further reverberations for the Commission. In 1993 Engler had named Chuck Yob, Republican National Committeeman from Michigan, to the Commission. Seeking to capitalize on the Kelley retirement, Engler recruited Scott Romney, son of the former governor and brother to future presidential candidate Mitt Romney, to be the GOP nominee when the party met in its late August 1998 convention. The Democratic nominee for Attorney General was widely expected to be Jennifer Granholm, an in-house attorney for Wayne County. Engler, like many other political observers, believed that if she won that office in November she would be the odds-on favorite to be a very formidable Democratic choice for governor in 2002. Thus, beating Jennifer Granholm was a high priority for Engler, and in Scott Romney he thought he had just the man to do it.

Yob, however, until that point a staunch Engler ally, decided to throw his political heft at the convention behind his long-time friend John Smietanka in opposition to Romney. To everyone's astonishment, Smietanka nosed out Romney for the nomination. Engler was furious, the more so when – as he predicted – Smietanka lost the November election to Granholm, for whom the 2002 stage was now set. When Yob's term on the Commission expired in April 1999 Engler did not re-appoint him. Yob came back onto the Commission in 2011, appointed by Gov. Rick Snyder who came into office at the end of Jennifer Granholm's eight years as Governor.

Engler also appointed another prominent Democrat to the Commission, again with an eye on the broader political picture. J. Bob Traxler was a U.S. Congressman for 18 years, including a stint as chair of a very powerful sub-committee of Appropriations. After leaving Washington he was elected to the Michigan State University Board of Trustees. I had, of course, known Traxler and been a good friend since we served together in the State House in the late 1960s and early 1970s. Engler, an MSU grad, badly wanted to exert his influence on MSU affairs and, Republicans being in a 4-3 minority on the Board of Trustees, he was just one trustee away from achieving his dream. Traxler, in turn, was growing restive on the MSU Board and privately very critical of its administration.

Engler saw his opportunity. If Traxler could be induced to resign and Engler able to name a Republican to the vacancy, Engler ally David Porteous could become MSU Board Chair. Since Porteous' wife was on the Mackinac commission by virtue of an earlier Engler appointment, if she would conveniently resign the way would be open to a Traxler appointment to the Mackinac Commission. The Mackinac appointment was dangled

Gov. Jennifer Granholm stands between the alternating chairmen. After my being Commission chairman for 16 years, Gov. Granholm reappointed me as a member in 2007 but asked that I step aside so a Democrat could serve as chairman. My law partner Frank Kelley thus moved into the position, but graciously stepped aside for me to return as chairman when a Republican was elected governor in 2010. My service as Chairman totaled eighteen and a half years and ended in April 2013.

before Traxler in the Fall of 2000 and the former Island busboy obligingly announced his resignation from the MSU Board. Engler promptly named a Republican to fill his position, the Board majority shifted to the Republicans, David Porteous became MSU Board Chair, and Traxler got his Mackinac commissionership, all in one fell swoop. At the next vacancy, Ms. Porteous was re-appointed back to the Commission by Engler. Democrats were not amused. When Traxler's term on the Commission expired during the Democratic Granholm Administration, he was not reappointed.

Through all of this partisan turmoil spanning two Administrations and sixteen years, I managed to survive as a Commissioner, helped by the statutory requirement of bi-partisanship and my status as Mackinac's "resident commissioner." It was not a clean sweep, however. After being re-appointed by Engler in 1995 and 2001, my term was set to expire in 2007 in a Granholm Administration. I was fairly confident of re-appointment, in part due to the staunch support of my law partner Frank Kelley whom Granholm always described as her political mentor. She called me to offer me re-appointment to another six-year term but made it clear that she expected me to relinquish the chairmanship to a Democrat whom, she confided, she expected would be Frank Kelley.

At the Commission's July 2007 meeting I duly stepped aside after 16 years in the chair and became the vice-chair. Frank Kelley was selected by Commission Democrats to be the new chair. The paper files of the chairman were duly shipped ten feet away to Frank Kelley's office adjoining my office at the Kelley Cawthorne law firm. There they would remain for the next three and a half years until Republican Rick Snyder was elected Governor, Kelley consequently resigning in favor of his vice-chair, the same person who had occupied the chairmanship prior to July 2007. The paper files of the outgoing chairman were duly shipped ten feet back the other direction. I would serve again as chair for the next two and a quarter years.

During my time on the Commission, we had many dedicated members. Richard Manoogian generously donated his own private funds to acquire land conservation easements, save other critical properties, and create a splendid art museum in the old Indian Dormitory. Joan Porteous helped convince trustees of the State Land Trust Fund to assist with land acquisitions. Ken Teysen and Audrey Jaggi, representing Mackinaw City, rallied that community behind various Commission efforts. Barry Goodman, a Granholm appointee and former president of the powerful Michigan Trial Lawyers Association, together with Laurie Stupak, helped garner Democratic support in the Legislature for the Commission's appropriations needs. She and her husband, U.S. Representative Bart Stupak, also brought in valuable federal assistance to Commission projects. Father Jim Williams, appointed by Granholm as Mackinaw City's representative, brought a "little man's" perspective to the Commission, sometimes served as its conscience, and played a vital role in issues involving repatriation of Native American remains.

And for all their backgrounds as identifiable partisans, Commissioners Kelley, Traxler, and Goodman always acted as statesmen having Mackinac's interest their first priority. The same could be said of the Commissioners who were transitioning out as I was coming on to that body: Pat McTigue, Nino Green, Kathy Lewand, Erica Ward, and Bruce Osterink.

David Armour, longtime deputy director and twice the acting director of Mackinac State Historic Parks, receives congratulations from Phil Porter (R) and Commissioner Jim Williams (L) at the opening of the Mill Creek Park Visitors Center named in his honor. Porter, a state park employee since his Kenyon College days and greatly respected in the Mackinac community, despite having to make hard decisions, became director in 2003.

Park Directors

When I first came to the Island, the job of running the Mackinac Island State Park Commission was bifurcated. Day to day park operations were handled as they had been since 1945 by the very capable Carl Nordberg. A second lead position, that of running the new revenue bond program that would refurbish Fort Mackinac and other state historical structures, was that of Director of Historic Projects. That slot was given to Dr. Eugene Petersen, an ex-college professor and well-regarded historian who had previously headed the Michigan Historical Museum in Lansing. His office manager, functioning as his right hand, was his capable wife Marian. After several years of two-headed administration and growing tension between the two, power was consolidated in Petersen's hands as Superintendent (later called Director) of the State Park. Nordberg, relegated to a subsidiary position and ill, soon retired.

Gene Petersen, who I got to know early in my Chamber days, was the guiding light and leader of the Commission staff. Petersen, often an idealist and ever the scholar, faced a formidable task in dragging along an inward-looking Commission and a frequently skeptical local community. But he persevered and under his leadership, in addition to the total refurbishment of Fort Mackinac and other Island historical structures, Fort Michillimackinac was re-created, all exhibits, programs, and research greatly enhanced, and Mackinac generally polished to a high gloss of historical restoration and scholarship.

When Petersen retired in 1985, the new Blanchard-appointed Commission decided it wanted new blood and, after 27 years, a fresh perspective. Thus, despite the excellent credentials of Petersen's long-time deputy Dr. David Armour, the Commission chose David Pamperin, a Wisconsin museum administrator, to take over the Superintendent's position. After six years, just months after I became Commission chair and unconnected to that event, Pamperin announced his resignation. Again, Dave Armour, who had continued and rendered loyal service as deputy under Pamperin, seemed in many ways a logical choice. The passage of time, however, had brought him closer to his inevitable retirement and the Commission opted to go with a younger candidate.

Carl Nold, director of the State Museum of Pennsylvania, was also an historian with excellent administrative credentials, and the Commission officially appointed him in the Fall of 1992. I thought Nold did an excellent job and we got along well, but it was also unfortunately true that he had his detractors both on staff and in the community.

As news circulated of Nold's intended departure in April 2003, many staffers, cottagers, and locals contacted me to urge selection of Phil Porter as the new director. They needn't have. His time to become leader of our operations had clearly come and we only perfunctorily interviewed other candidates. Porter, with strong local roots and a grandfather who had served on the Commission, had been with the Park since college days and had ably worked his way up through the ranks. Possessed of good academic credentials, he was the Commission's unanimous choice in the early Fall of 2003.

My relationship with Porter was consistently strong, at least in my eyes. He had not only an encyclopedic knowledge of Commission history, workings, and procedures but also had good political sense and enjoyed the respect and trust of the local community. I made it a point to stay out of the daily workings of the staff and its director and believed in letting them do their work free of interference, especially of the political kind. My job and that of all Commissioners, I believed, was to set broad policy and lend local support to the achievement of all Commission goals.

This view had not always been that of past Commissioners or Chairs. During the depths of the Depression, Commission Chair Roger Andrews also took on the task of running routine operations in place of a paid Superintendent. All during Bill Doyle's tenure as Chair, he insisted that the Commission was a "working commission," thus justifying using for Commissioners all Commission resources—housing, personnel, and carriages with drivers—to the fullest extent possible. Later, Director Gene Petersen appreciated the hands-off professionalism of Chairman Sheldon Smith when he served from 1975 to 1983, but Smith's successor William Ellman (1983-85) regularly drove director and staff to distraction by popping into Commission offices at all hours of the day and attempting every type of micromanagement. In desperation, Petersen reportedly installed an advance warning system so that at the first sight of Ellman trudging in their direction, staff could take whatever defensive steps were required.

In the last decade, under Director Porter, the Commission's Education Outreach program was expanded, strategic long-range plans developed, the Old Mackinac Point Lighthouse re-opened, the Richard and Jane Manoogian Art Museum opened, and Historic Mill Creek Discovery Park created in a re-branding of that site. During that same time, Mackinac Island was named by the National Geographic Society as one of the top ten state parks in the country and the Island selected as one of "America's Dozen Distinctive Destinations for Historic Preservation."

Through the years, the Commission has been singularly fortunate in having directors of the caliber of Petersen, Armour, Pamperin, Nold, and Porter. That it has had only five directors in 55 years is remarkable and a testament to the quality of their services

Changing of the guard. New State Park Director David Pamperin chats with Dr. Eugene Petersen, his predecessor, at the opening of the new Fort Michillimackinac exhibit in 1989. In the background, future director Phil Porter.

In 1993 incoming Director Carl Nold (left) takes the reins from interim Director David Armour who served as Acting Director on three different occasions in the space between 1982 and 2003

The Detroit News AND Free Press

Sunday, January 5, 1992 — $1.25

Leasing state land on Mackinac a sweet deal

■ **Subsidy:** Critics say thousands in taxes lost on rock-bottom arrangements for pricey cottages' lots.

By Jim Mitzelfeld
DETROIT NEWS LANSING BUREAU

LANSING — Michigan is charging owners of 35 spacious and expensive Victorian cottages built on state-owned land on Mackinac Island an average of just $51 a year to lease their prime, lake-view lots.

In what amounts to a state subsidy for some fortunate everyday people, as well as some of the region's richest and most prominent citizens, the practice has gone virtually unnoticed since Michigan inherited the island park from the federal government in 1895.

The state owns the land, but has allowed individuals to lease portions of it and build summer homes, some with as many as 26 rooms and sale prices of more than $2 million.

Critics say the cheap leases are robbing the state of thousands of dollars in revenue at a time Gov. John Engler is trimming welfare rolls and looking for dollars to balance the state budget.

The nominal lease rates, ranging from $20 to $160 a year, were increased last fall for the first time in a half-century by the seven-member Mackinac Island State Park Commission. During the 50-year price freeze, inflation shot up 600 percent.

The small increase in lease fees hasn't stopped some from questioning whether it is wise for Michigan's governors to appoint cottage owners to sit on the commission that determines lease rates.

Some argue the state should be charging cottage owners between $1,000 and $10,000 a year if it is to get a fair return on the land's value.

"It's terrible," said state Rep. Margaret O'Connor, the Ann Arbor Republican who has become a lead critic of what

Please see Land, 10A

Highlights
■ Critics say a fair return on leases would be between $1,000 and $10,000.
■ Owners pay taxes only on their homes, most of which are under-assessed.

On Page 10A
■ Most owners admit they're getting a great deal.
■ Former Gov. Milliken got latest lease in 1983.

BLAKE J. DISCHER

The Great Lease Wars of 1991-1994

One of the Mackinac Island State Park Commission's major responsibilities involves setting terms and conditions for leasing to private parties 38 desirable parcels of land located within the State Park. On these properties sit most of the Island's finest summer homes, architectural gems constructed in the late 19th century and early 20th century, mostly on the high bluffs west of Grand Hotel and east of Fort Mackinac. The lands are state-owned and thus exempt from local property taxes, but they are leased to persons who build private residences which are subject to personal property taxes and payment of a state rental fee for the leased land under them.

The federal government first started leasing these lands and scattered other parcels as a means of generating revenue for park improvements in the new National Park. The first cottage was built in 1885 on the East Bluff, and in the next fifteen or so years virtually all of the spectacular sites were built upon. When the State of Michigan took over the park from the federal government in 1895, Commissioners retained the lease program but doubled the annual rentals to $100 and cut lease terms in half to five years.

A third of a century later, in the Depression of the 1930s, many leases went into default for non-payment of rents and a number of cottages reverted to the State for non-payment of property taxes. Summer homes could be bought for $300 to $2500 apiece. Still others were simply boarded up. In response, the Commission slashed rates by 60% in 1939 and by another 50% in 1942. From 1942 to 1992, a half century, rents were never raised from these rock bottom levels even though the selling prices of many of these homes soared after World War II, exceeding in many cases one and two million dollars. Thus, when I came onto the Commission in 1991 some of the most beautiful and desirable homes in the entire Midwest sat on land for which cottage owners were paying an annual rent of $25, $50, and $75. In the case of the Mackinac Island Yacht Club the rent for their leased land was exactly one dollar.

In my view, not only was that grossly unfair to the State and its citizens, it was a political time bomb. Yes, most cottagers had lovingly protected their Victorian-era cottages and spent large sums of money to maintain them. But I also believed that if and when the general public found out (though it was technically not a secret), they would demand radical reform that would rock state government, the Commission, and even cottage owners themselves.

Almost immediately, however, I became concerned that we needed to be more aggressive and I was preparing to ask the Commission to take strong steps when *The Detroit News* and *Free Press* (published jointly on Sundays) in its January 5, 1992 edition carried a screaming front page headline, "Leasing State Land on Mackinac A Sweet Deal." Fat cat millionaires, it said, were paying $50 a year for sites of million dollar homes. Jumping into the fray, Tom Washington, the sometimes bombastic executive director of the 135,000 member Michigan United Conservation Clubs said, "The people of the state are being ripped off." Soon a handful of legislators were also baying along the trail.

At our regular Commission meeting five days later on January 10, I asked the Commission to take action. I knew from my legislative experience that to mollify both leaseholders and a skeptical public, it would be far better if the Commission could point to an unbiased study and recommendations from an independent group as justification for jacking up rates to the proper levels. From my legislative days I also knew it was possible to "guide" an independent body to the desired result and, to do so, it was highly important that the "right" people do the study and make the recommendations.

When I proposed creation of a "Blue Ribbon Advisory Board" to examine and make recommendations for change, the Commission unanimously agreed. Its membership was very carefully chosen. I asked to serve as chairman Philip E. Runkel, former State Superintendent of Public Instruction, now vice-president of a small securities firm, and the owner of a condominium unit on non-state land. Phil Runkel, I knew, was politically savvy and could be trusted to mold and shape the panel's final recommendations in a way that met my objectives while giving the report a scholarly, high level of credibility with the public and the media. Runkel's Lansing office was fortunately in the same downtown building as that of my law office and we talked frequently behind the scenes during the panel's deliberations and before the panel's report was released in draft form in May 1992.

The other members of the panel also proved to be excellent choices who took their task seriously. They included Commissioner Steve Vogel, a historical architect who was also chair of the Detroit Historic District Commission and loyal to me for having him appointed by Governor Engler to the State Park Commission; George Yshinski, a St. Ignace realtor

Philip Runkel

who would give area-wide credibility to the group's work; Jennifer Radcliff, president of the Michigan Historical Preservation Network; Kathryn Beebe, director of real estate for a major Detroit accounting firm; Joseph Schmidt, an Island aficionado and chair of the Midland (Michigan) Planning Commission; and retired Circuit Judge Edward Fenlon of Petoskey, highly regarded in the Straits area and, in his youth during Prohibition, widely alleged to be a rum runner between Canada and the Island.

News that the Commission was getting serious about land lease reform sent up howls of protest from leaseholders, especially those from the East Bluff. Chief among the protestors were two retired state appellate court judges, Glenn Allen and John Fitzgerald, both of whom also had long and distinguished careers in partisan politics at both the local and state levels. I was frankly astounded that, given their political experience, they could be tone-deaf to the mounting public clamor for reform. Pressure mounted even more when the House Fiscal Agency, a non-partisan agency of the Legislature, mid-way in the Blue Ribbon's deliberations, issued scathing criticism of the existing system. Still the cottagers demurred.

To ensure adequate public input, the Blue Ribbon panel scheduled public hearings over a two day period in June. Nervous leaseholders turned out in large numbers to make their case before the body. The essence of their argument was that maintenance costs for the cottages were high and that the new lease rates on top of that would force many to sell their cottages. Images of the dark days of the 1930s were conjured and dire predictions made of cottagers selling en masse and property values plummeting. That it had been sixty years or more since the Great Depression, that times had changed, and bluff houses were now selling for one and two million dollars apiece was left unsaid.

Edward Fenlon

John Fitzgerald

The panel's report, when issued in July after two days of public hearings, was a highly professional, carefully reasoned analysis which acknowledged the contributions to the Island and its ambience by lease holders but which also recognized the equity of a greatly revised rental schedule. Specifically, it recommended a $3500 annual rent for West Bluff cottages also having carriage houses and/or stables; $2500 for all other West Bluff cottages and all East Bluff and Fort Garden cottages; and $1000 for all other cottages. Rents would be adjusted annually to reflect changes in the Consumer Price Index.

Glen Allen

Because rents could change only upon lease transfers or expiration, it was recognized that it would take twenty years for the new schedule to be fully implemented. Put another way, some leaseholders would continue to enjoy rock bottom rents for the next nineteen years, and some of our most vocal critics were in that number.

Now the action shifted to the Commission. At a meeting held August 29, 1992, at Mission Point Resort to accommodate an overflow crowd, Commissioners heard additional public testimony. Most leaseholders, of course, were unhappy in the extreme with the panel's recommendations, and the arguments heard at the June public hearings were made once more before the Commission. At meeting's end, Commissioners voted 5 to 1, with one abstention, to adopt the Blue Ribbon recommendations "as a basis or benchmark" for considering future lease terms.

Commissioner Richard Kughn, himself a West Bluff leaseholder, had announced in advance that he would abstain to prevent a conflict of interest, but he also indicated in public that he generally supported the Blue Ribbon recommendations. Commissioner Meg Brown, the Commission vice-chair, however, gave no advance indication that she would oppose the Blue Ribbon recommendations. I was highly disappointed that, but for her surprise "no" vote, we would have had a united front on a contentious issue calling for Commission solidarity.

The last issues on the Commission agenda were two lease renewals and one lease transfer. Within minutes the Commission exercised its new authority by approving $3500 a year 20-year leases for George Burrows, Richard Kughn, and John Barr, all of the West Bluff. True lease reform had at last been achieved.

The battle was not over, however. Three weeks later, on September 18, the newly formed Mackinac Island Leaseholders' Association and 31 of 38 leaseholders filed suit against the Commission in Ingham County Circuit Court. Their claim was that the Commission had illegally adopted the new rent schedule and had done so without adequate public input. The Commission's attorney, the Office of the Attorney General, dismissed the leaseholders' claim of illegal adoption as plainly wrong, and the fact the Blue Ribbon panel and the Commission had together heard two and a half days of public testimony blew apart the leaseholders' second objection.

It was my opinion, however, that the leaseholders did have one valid concern and that was the open-endedness of the Consumer Price Index adjustment that would each year change the amount of rent owed. As the leaseholder suit plodded on through the courts in the winter of 1992-93, I held several informal meetings with the leaseholder leadership (with the knowledge and consent of counsel). In May 1993 we reached an agreement. The most important point of the accord was to cap the CPI adjustment in any one year at 5% and over the life of a 20 year lease at 225% compounded. The Commission formally approve the revision at its July 10 meeting and by stipulation the suit was dropped shortly after.

When at last the dust finally settled, two other provisions of the Blue Ribbon report adopted by the Commission began to be noticed by concerned parties. One was that changes to the exterior of homes on leased lands would need to get Commission approval in the future and must meet the U.S. Secretary of Interior's "Standards for Rehabilitation." This marked a major step forward in responsible preservation and its impact has been felt well into the 21st century.

The other important provision was a requirement that sellers of homes on leased land file an affidavit of sale price thus greatly aiding the local assessor in establishing fair and accurate taxable values. *The Detroit News* and the *Detroit Free Press* had both criticized the low valuations the City had placed on homes located on leased lands and had correctly observed that much of the problem was due to a lack of adequate information on which to base assessments. The new reporting requirement predictably had the effect of substantially increasing most Bluff home taxes but, as in the case of the increased lease rates, the end result was equitable and just.

Echoes of the controversy could be heard a year later and beyond. Columnist George Weeks of the *Detroit News* provided a summary of the controversy, and I derived a measure of satisfaction when he wrote, "Cawthorne…correctly said the Commission had to act because 'the public would not have tolerated the status quo on rock bottom fees for leaseholder of land.'"

Still not letting the matter rest, the September 15, 1994 *Detroit News* carried a large spread on page one of its Michigan section entitled, "Anger on Mackinac Island," featuring photos of leaseholders Jim Dunnigan and Bill Porter. The article said Cawthorne was "pitted against…the Mackinac Island Leaseholders Association" and quoted me as saying "Mackinac wouldn't be Mackinac without at least three major controversies going at once."

The balance of the lengthy article set forth the emerging grievances of three leaders of the Leaseholders Association who claimed that the Commission had "created a terrible wrench for families facing huge lease fees," and "the Commission (isn't) the least bit interested in assuring that moderate-income families are able to keep their homes." After two and a half years and reams of publicity, it was clear that not everyone yet recognized the public's stake in the matter: its right to receive fair compensation for the use of public resources.

Said Weeks, "As the debate rages, Cawthorne, former Republican leader in the State House, reflected that 'the politics (on Mackinac) are at least equal to anything found under the Capital dome.'"

Yacht Club: A Dollar Doesn't Go As Far As It Used To

The controversy over land leases was not completely settled, however, for another 20 years. Unresolved was the issue of the lease held by the Mackinac Island Yacht Club, formed in 1937 and headquartered in a house located near downtown on state land.

At the time of the original media blast over leases in 1991, the Yacht Club had just months before been granted a new 20 year one-dollar-a-year lease. This had occurred just before I came on the Commission. That lease was the one that most leaped out at the press and public when the controversy got hot.

On Mackinac, even normally sleepy institutions like its yacht club, can get caught up in controversy. *The Detroit News* had the club in its sights in 1991.

Adding fuel to the fire, the *Detroit News* made much of the fact that there were no blacks among its 238 members. When pressed as to why, Yacht Club Commodore Mick Caulkins denied any discriminatory intent, but added, "My guess is that most of (our) members don't socialize with blacks." Kathy Lewand, chair of the Commission when the latest dollar a year lease was granted, was more direct in rebutting the *News'* inferences: "No blacks have ever applied. They don't have any green Martians in the Club either."

It began to appear to me that there was perhaps a political agenda behind the newspaper attacks and that was to embarrass the new Engler Administration. This, even though the abuses, if that's what they were, had occurred in prior administrations and even though the new Commission leadership was committed to fixing the problem well before the press had seized on the issue. I was highly reluctant to criticize past Commissions but I did think it was essential that Engler and the incumbent Commission be protected from unfair attacks. Accordingly, the *News* reported that Cawthorne said he "would never have agreed to (the $1 lease)" and "said if he finds any proof the club discriminates against minorities he would personally ask the state attorney general to vigorously pursue the matter."

When the Blue Ribbon panel issued its report in August 1992 it reserved special criticism for the Yacht Club lease. The State Auditor General's office jumped in shortly

Bart Huthwaite, summer resident, Yacht Club commodore before its lease controversy, and unpaid author of the popular Dock Lines column in the Island's *Town Crier*. He led the effort to restore the Bernida, winner of the first Port Huron to Mackinac Yacht Race in 1925.

thereafter with its own negative comments. I responded by asking the Attorney General's office if there might be a flaw in the Club's new lease that might give us cause to invalidate it rather than having to wait nearly twenty years for its expiration. Possibly, was the response, but not substantial enough to warrant another long legal fight.

I then suggested that maybe the Yacht Club's members might want to be "good citizens" and voluntarily agree to a new rate schedule. That went nowhere, perhaps because it was thought by Club members that by waiting another 20 years they could outlast members of the then-current commission.

Thus the Commission bided its time…for the next 19 years. The year before the $1 lease was to expire, I asked the Commission staff to inform the Yacht Club that we would be seeking a major revision in rent so they could begin to plan their dues and finances accordingly. I also noted that the Commission was not necessarily bound by the existing top rate since that applied to residential land and not to the Yacht Club's commercial usage.

The reaction of the Club's leadership, however, was reminiscent of the cottagers' protests back in 1991-1994. (And here we thought this battle had been settled 20 years before!) The Yacht Club Commodore first claimed that their lease had somehow automatically renewed for another 20 years and at a dollar a year. When that didn't fly, the club sought to postpone any rate hike for a year. When the Club's leadership delayed signing a one year lease extension (pending determination of an exact new rate), the Commission rattled the saber of ejectment from the premises. It didn't take long for the Club leadership to see the light.

At our next meeting, in May 2010, the Commission granted, and the Club accepted, a new 20-year lease, not for $1 a year as had been the case since 1937, but $8,500 a year. According to my calculations, a dues increase of less than $38 per member annually would cover any rent increase.

For the record, I myself was a member of the Club back in 1963 when dues were $50 a year, and I always recognized that the Yacht Club and its members, most of whom were from off the Island, had made many valuable contributions to the Community. That, however, did not alter my view that the Commission's very substantial rate revision was the right thing to do.

Land Theft . . . and Redemption

When MRA, or more precisely Mackinac College, folded in 1970, its property was acquired the next year by televangelist Rex Humbard whose Ohio-based Cathedral of Tomorrow's services were carried by 355 television stations in the United States and Canada.

Humbard had two goals for his Mackinac property: to re-open Mackinac College as a non-denominational Bible college and to turn Stonecliffe into a winter ski resort. In the fall of 1972 the second Mackinac College opened with 140 students. At Stonecliffe he constructed a faux-Alpine ski lodge adjacent to the old mansion. On the Island's far west side he cleared strips of wooded bluff lands and constructed ski slopes which at their bottom crossed M-185 and ended in a newly-filled portion of Lake Huron (contrary to state law regarding such fills). The ski runs operated a grand total of one day. After its first day, the westward-facing slope was swept bare by prevailing winds, and the tiny amount of snow that was left melted in the sun that beat directly on it and then turned into ice. The gash created by the clearing of the slopes remains visible to this day.

Failure of the ski venture proved to be the least of Humbard's problems. His empire was soon engulfed in financial crisis, and by the spring of its first year the second Mackinac College closed its doors. With Humbard's exit, the Island's usually tight real estate market was suddenly awash with excess property. All the old Mission district cottages originally acquired by MRA were available at bargain prices, as were units in the new Lesley Court condominiums plus Stonecliffe and the large tracts of land surrounding it. For anyone with a few extra dollars in his pocket, which at that time did not include me, the Island offered much opportunity.

The main property at Mission Point, consisting of the Great Hall, theatre, library, dormitories, and classrooms, soon caught the eye of would-be hoteliers. Though the cost of conversion to hotel-ready status would be great, the basic purchase price seemed a bargain at a little over $2 million. A succession of hotel owners tried their luck over the next decade and more before the properties were finally acquired by John Shufelt who had made a small fortune in the

I was pleased to have been recognized for my efforts to preserve these and other beautiful and sensitive Island lands. Pictured left to right, Brevin Cawthorne, Cynthia Cawthorne, grandchildren Tyler and Kaden, and Dennis Cawthorne.

software industry. Cottages in the Mission were quickly snapped up and units at Lesley Court sold for as little as $28,000 each.

Stonecliffe was another matter. In 1974, while still a member of the legislature, I urged Governor Milliken and the State Park Commission to acquire the property and add it to the State Park. That idea went nowhere. Shortly afterward a downstate mortician-turned-developer, George Staffan, put together a group for Stonecliffe's purchase. Staffan was soon at work planning development of the property on a large scale. He was plagued almost from the beginning with foreclosures, threats of foreclosures and far too little capital, but he persisted and eventually a community began to arise on the extensive acreage surrounding the old mansion.

Then in 1982 he hit pay dirt, literally. The Mackinac County Circuit Court ruled that his company, Mackinac Island Development Company, Ltd., had acquired by adverse possession 36.6 acres of land, including 2,250 feet of Lake Huron frontage on the west side of the island below Stonecliffe. Back in 1923 the State Park Commission had expanded the park by over fifty percent by acquiring 612 acres from John and Peter Early. At the same time it also bought a 43/63 interest in this same 36.6 acre parcel. In 1965 the Commission inexplicably failed to assert its rights when MRA, owner of the remaining 20/63, brought suit against the State for damage the property sustained in an airport construction project. The door was open to Staffan, MRA's successor in interest, to bring an action for adverse possession.

Suddenly, Staffan's empire was much larger and far more valuable. Jubilation surely prevailed in the Staffan household when, the following year, the State Court of Appeals upheld the circuit court decision and the State Supreme Court refused to hear further appeals.

How a claim for adverse possession can prevail against the sovereign, i.e., the State of Michigan, especially if the subject property is publicly-used park lands, is a mystery that will baffle most lawyers. That was especially so here because the state acknowledged that the plaintiff already had an undivided 20/63 interest in the property, something which would explain why MRA's presence on the property – along with the general public's – was neither adverse nor hostile, two of the key elements necessary to perfect a claim for "adverse possession."

Staffan, meanwhile, soon ran into more financial problems. Now, as a private citizen, I contacted him to ask what it would take for the State to re-acquire the 36.6 acres. Three hundred thousand dollars, he said, and I again asked the State Park Commission to find the money and make the purchase. Again, nothing happened.

At some point in the late 1980s, the 36.6 acres with its nearly half-mile of Lake Huron frontage was sold by a bankruptcy court—for a fraction of its real worth—to Manthei Development Corporation of Charlevoix and Petoskey. This would potentially open the way to clear cutting and extensive development of nearly one-half mile of road frontage on what had been nearly three miles of pristine woods and water extending from the end of the boardwalk below Grand Hotel to a point just south of British Landing. My worst fears for this pristine property were, it appeared, about to come true.

On February 28, 1991 I became chairman of the same Commission which years earlier had turned a deaf ear to my pleas for taking the land back into the protection of the State Park. At that meeting I put on the record one of my chief goals as Commission chair: "Vigorous action to return to public ownership, if at all possible, over 36 acres of unique shoreland property lost through adverse judicial decisions." I would now have the chance to have the Commission do what previous commissions had failed to do: retrieve some of the lost lands.

So began a long, slow process. The Commission proceeded on two fronts: first to get quid pro quo concessions from Manthei for things it needed to go forward with development, second to obtain state monies to purchase outright key parcels adjacent to Brown's Brook, the one piece of the 40-acre parcel that the Court ruled was not subject to the adverse possession. (Hence the net 36.6 acres going to Staffan and, ultimately, Manthei).

After protracted negotiations also involving the City of Mackinac Island, in exchange for needed sewer and water services for 27 homesites, Manthei agreed to deed 125 feet of beachfront property to the State Park and to create a scenic reserve easement – a strip of land the length of the property from Lake Huron to 55 feet east of the center of Lake Shore Boulevard or "to the brow of the first ridge whichever is less." In this space, tree removal would be sharply restricted in recognition of the Commission's concern that future lot owners would clear cut on either side of the road. I was pleased at the protection promised but feared that the enforcement mechanisms were far too weak. Twenty years into the development, I can say that some of my and the Commission's worst fears did not materialize and that most of the homes constructed on the Manthei property were of good quality, suitable appearance, and built with relatively few trees destroyed.

In late 1996 the Commission gained title to still more land south of Brown's Brook and obtained scenic easements over an additional 150 feet along the shore road. In 1998 the Commission purchased another 214 feet in the area, and it was satisfying to now see significant tangible progress in preserving the beauty of lands in and adjacent to the 36.6 acres.

The Commission also applied to the Natural Resources Trust Fund and was awarded money to acquire other small but important pieces. In addition, Commissioner Richard Manoogian personally paid for the acquisition of development rights on the north side of Brown's Brook. The net result was preservation of a good portion of land on both sides of its picturesque waters.

This did not end the Commission's quest for additional lands to preserve, one of my highest priorities as chairman. We received from Grand Hotel a scenic easement to preserve shorelands near the end of the boardwalk. We acquired development rights on 6 ½ acres of land near British Landing and, most importantly, we acquired Chimney Rock (sometimes called Sunset Rock), one of the most spectacular vistas on the Island. That purchase included over a half-acre of land and an easement for the public to access the tall limestone outcropping that overlooks the Straits and the Mackinac Bridge. And, once again,

Richard Manoogian stepped in with private funds to acquire and preserve from development another 18 acres of forest land near Chimney Rock.

One major land preservation project remained. In the 1980s, before I was a member of the Commission, acting as a private attorney I handled a series of land transactions between the State of Michigan and the owners of Mission Point. Those dealings made me acutely aware of the fact that, despite all outward appearances to the contrary, the resort was actually land-locked. It owned no waterfront, but frequently used the shoreland fronting the hotel as if it did.

This brought back vivid memories of the 36.6-acre land theft in 1983. Now, in 1998 as Commission chair, I was determined to not let history repeat itself. The lands in front of Mission Point needed to be permanently identified as state property and demarcated as such. The 2,400 foot water front was state-owned, but not by the Commission as in the case of all other state lands on the Island. Rather, title was in the State Waterways Commission which had earlier hoped to construct a marina on the property. My first objective was to convince Waterways to turn the shoreland over to the Commission, but that effort went nowhere. As an alternative, I asked Waterways to allow the Commission to construct and oversee a paved bike path that would traverse the entire length of the State shoreland property fronting Mission Point Resort. It would, I noted, provide cyclists with panoramic views of Round Island Lighthouse, Robinson's Folly, Hiawatha National Forest, and freighter traffic through the Straits.

Twice the project nearly blew up. The City interpreted changes in the original route plan as somehow opening the door to construction of a new marina, which it did not, and John Shufelt, who had become owner of Mission Point subsequent to my earlier work as a private attorney, voiced concerns over design and materials for the project. Fortunately, these obstacles were soon removed, and on Memorial Day weekend 1999 the trail was opened to the public. In some respects, this beautiful project was one of my proudest accomplishments as Park Commission chair. Counting the shoreline trail, I can say—objectively, I think—my efforts at shoreline preservation resulted in nearly one mile of Lake Huron frontage being preserved or protected for the public's use.

As for Stonecliffe, the ski lodge was sold to Grand Hotel and became a restaurant known as The Woods. Grand also purchased the golf course George Staffan had started to construct north of the mansion. Today it is the "back nine" of Grand Hotel's links. Condominium units were built overlooking the Straits just west of the mansion. Homes sprouted up in a subdivision known as Sunset Forest and along the fairways of the new back nine. Today, after 30 years, the area is the substantial, contained community that George Staffan envisioned but in his time never fully realized.

Wings Over Mackinac

Over the years, Mackinac Island's airport, located on a plateau high above the downtown, has been both a lifeline and a lightning rod. When ferries aren't running, in winter and after 11 p.m. in summer, air transport is the only means off the Island for those in emergency need. The extent to which that air traffic should be aided, abetted, and enhanced by physical improvements, however, has been a subject of Island controversy ever since the first plane landed on Mackinac in the 1920s.

In 1934 laborers of the Depression-era Works Progress Administration (WPA) constructed an 1800 foot grassy landing strip over an abandoned dump. In winter, large bonfires adjacent to the strip, tended by one or two men from Harrisonville, kept passengers warm until they could depart on a rickety single engine plane. Many locals, fearing the disturbance and increased traffic of an upgraded facility, opposed any talk of improvement.

By 1963, however, in my second year at the Chamber of Commerce, it had become clear that the strip was not only inadequate but unsafe. The City of Mackinac Island proposed that the State Park Commission lease to it land sufficient for a 3500-foot paved runway that could accommodate planes as large as a DC-3. The State Aeronautics Commission, which had originally proposed the upgrade, enthusiastically supported the project and stepped in with three quarters of the funding. Many locals, however, were opposed to even this project on grounds of noise and a general aversion to anything that could detract from the horse-and-buggy tranquility of their beloved island. Ultimately, the proponents prevailed.

The new airstrip was dedicated on August 14, 1965, amid much fanfare but not before the City backed out of operating the property. "I don't know that the City could afford five or six thousand dollars a year (to operate) the airstrip," Councilman John Bloswick said. Operational responsibility of the new facility thus passed into the hands of the State Park Commission which, in any event, already owned the land occupied by the airport.

Though there was a new paved airstrip, the Commission quickly recognized that much more was needed. Accordingly, it set about making plans for a small terminal building, a full time on-site operator, tie downs, fencing, and on-ground radio controls.

In the next few years all became a reality. In the ensuing years, air traffic to the Island increased exponentially, and many people were surprised to learn that traffic was heaviest in the months of January and February when, absent an ice bridge, the only transport of people, groceries, and supplies was by air. In 1995 nearly 14,000 take-offs and landings were recorded.

Despite a nearly spotless safety record over the years, a near-miss air tragedy involving Newt Gingrich, Speaker of the U.S. House of Representatives, thrust airport expansion back into the limelight in the summer of 1996. The previous September, after attending the biennial Michigan Republican Leadership Conference, Gingrich's small jet aborted takeoff when it ran into a flock of Canada Geese. The aircraft ran 30 feet off the runway, just short of a high cliff. One goose was sucked into the right engine, another dented the left wing.

That was enough to spur into action State Aeronautics Commissioner Alice Gustafson of Pontiac who announced she would push that body to expand the Mackinac strip to 4,300 feet and widen it from 75 feet to 100 feet. To accomplish this, however, the historic British Landing Road would have to be moved 600 feet to the east. Not surprisingly, this touched off a firestorm. When accused of using the Gingrich incident as a cover to open the Island airport to commercial services, Gustafson testily responded, "Safety, safety, safety. That's all this is about."

Gustafson, a millionaire beer distributor and political activist, had considerable sway with her fellow Aeronautics commissioners. She did not, however, count on the fact that there would have to be sign-off by the Mackinac Island State Park Commission, the airport's owner and operator. I was reluctant to dismiss out-of-hand the strong desires of another state commission, but I also knew that the local community was adamantly opposed to what it was trying to accomplish. When pressed by the media, my response was that I was opposed to anything that "jeopardizes the character of the Island."

At the Commission's July 27, 1996 meeting attended by over 100 people, I proposed creation of two study committees: one to study the Aeronautics plan by itself, the other to look at alternative safety improvements not utilizing an 800-foot runway extension. The Commission agreed and set a special public meeting for August 24 to make final determinations. Meantime, Commissioners L. Margaret (Meg) Brown and Mark Schlussel, who chaired the respective study committees, worked overtime to produce their reports.

In my mind, there was little doubt what our Commission should and would eventually do. The Gustafson forces had submitted voluminous petitions from pilots and others supporting her position. The local ad hoc citizens protest group, Mackinac Island

Citizens Against Runway Expansion (MI-CARE) submitted almost as many in opposition. The Commission wouldn't make its decision based on competing piles of petitions, I said, but I also recognized that local sentiment in the matter was overwhelmingly negative.

At our August special meeting a packed house heard Aeronautics Commissioner Gustafson make her pitch, and I felt a twinge of sympathy for her when the audience greeted her remarks with unconcealed hostility. On the other hand, I felt good knowing that the Commission's fore-ordained position would be to reject the expansion but take the $1.7 million Aeronautics had ear-marked for the project and use it for a raft of safety improvements recommended by the second study group. At the Aeronautics Commission meeting in November, that body approved nearly all the safety measures recommended by our Commission. By the spring of 1998 our safety project, fully funded by the Aeronautics Commission, was complete and in service.

"The issue," I told the press, "had an effect on unifying the whole community in a way we haven't seen in some time, and it raised the importance of continuously protecting the Island and the environment."

I felt a measure of satisfaction with the reaction of Maeve Croghan, co-chair of the local citizens group MI-CARE: "Everyone is thrilled at the outcome."

Major airport improvements, especially in lighting, were made in 1997-1998. Ten years later, in 2008 the airport terminal received a major $2.5 million renovation that also included additional runway lights and a weather tracking system. In winter, Islanders could now wait for planes in total comfort in a time and setting far distant from 1934 and the bonfires along a grassy strip.

In 2012 there occurred the most expensive capital project ever undertaken by the Mackinac Island State Park Commission. At a cost of $4.5 million, the airport makeover eliminated a dangerous and prominent hump in the runway and permanently remedied the problem of runway sinkholes in the vicinity of the old garbage dump. The runway was shifted slightly to the west, trees cleared, and all hard surfaces re-paved. When completed, Mackinac Island's airport could rightfully claim to be one of finest small airports in the Midwest.

Chamber of Commerce Board member Maria Moeller and the Chamber manager get set to welcome the Port Huron to Mackinac fleet at the downtown harbor, 1963

Whatever Floats Your Boat

The airport was not the only Island transportation link that would stir local and statewide controversy. The downtown marina, or yacht dock, roused even greater passion in a running battle that lasted a good part of 15 years.

Beginning in the 1920s the State Park Commission opened and operated a facility for small boats, but after World War II it realized that it had neither the money nor the expertise required for the rapidly expanding needs of the burgeoning boating community. The State Park Commission thereupon turned the facility over to the State Waterways Commission, a part of the Department of Natural Resources, which was clearly better equipped to fund and run it. A major expansion and improvement was undertaken in 1965 by Waterways, and as Chamber manager I was invited along with Gov. George Romney to speak at its dedication.

Six years after I left the legislature and after I had worked as a private attorney on an exchange of waterfront lands at Mission Point, the DNR decided a major expansion of facilities at Mackinac Island was overdue. In 1985 it proposed a second state marina at Mission Point that would accommodate 200 boats. The project foundered when the City objected in part because it had not been consulted on the ambitious plan.

In 1993 Waterways, declaring that Mackinac Island was the state's number one boating destination and that "one hundred boats are routinely crammed into space for only 77" at the existing marina, announced plans for a 30-slip addition there. At the same time Lynn Williams, an East Bluff cottager working with Mission Point owner John Shufelt, announced plans for 40 condo boat slips to be built on hotel property near the site of the old Beaver Dock. The state plan for the existing marina sank when adjacent property owners refused to give needed bottomlands rights and Williams' plan for Mission Point also petered out.

Only two years later, in 1995, controversy arose again when Waterways proposed a 48-foot addition to its comfort station at the existing marina. Adjacent property owners said the enlarged station with its higher roof line would ruin their view, and the City entered the fray by saying local zoning approval was needed. Governor Engler and DNR Director Rollie Harmes asked me if I could, as a private citizen and not as a State Park Commissioner, find a compromise solution, especially since all parties agreed that existing shower and toilet facilities were inadequate. Working with the lessees of Island House, I was successful in coming up with a very workable alternative. I was therefore astonished when the DNR rejected it without giving a reason. The comfort station, like the dock expansions, died a quiet death. At about the same time, the DNR also gave consideration to privatizing the marina and all its operations, but Attorney General Frank Kelley soon threw cold water on that.

By now the Department's patience with Mackinac Island and its marina was wearing thin, but that didn't stop it from making still another try at expanding the existing marina. This time the plan called for adding 50 slips at a cost of $5.4 million, but again no settlement could be reached with adjacent property owners and that project, too, hit a dead end.

In 1999 the DNR made one last grand effort. Flush with gas-tax monies, the Waterways Commission unveiled plans for a $15 million 122-slip marina adjacent to Mission Point. It would be complete with large new breakwalls and a clubhouse. The plan immediately touched off a firestorm, some of it fueled by East Bluff property owners who feared noise and perhaps other detrimental effects, some by strict preservationists, and some by those instinctively opposed to anything that would benefit Mission Point Resort. It didn't help that once again the City felt left out of the DNR's process.

My own view was that a properly conceived project could be a real plus for the Island. I was not a boat owner, and thus had no direct stake in the matter, but it did seem that some measure of expanded facilities would attract the kind of demographic that would enhance the Island's efforts to attract quality shops and the kind of people who would support new artistic and cultural programs then getting traction on the Island.

Opponents of the latest Waterways plan pushed the State Park Commission to take a stand against it, but we pointed out that—unlike the airport—the Commission had no jurisdiction in the matter. As Commissioner Mark Schlussel said, "The Park Commission was able to thwart the airport effort because we viewed that as another commission interfering with the activities of the Mackinac State Park Commission. It would be the ultimate act of hypocrisy if now the Park Commission was to interfere with the activities of the Waterways Commission."

Whether the new Mission Point project was too grandiose and encroaching was certainly open to question, however, and the Waterways Commission, beaten down again for the fifteenth year running, came back with yet another scaled-down version. It was to no avail. Tired of the battle, Waterways redirected a good portion of the money to marinas in Mackinaw City and St. Ignace where the State's largesse was eagerly accepted.

In 2010 a new comfort station adjacent to the existing marina was finally erected. Marina expansion itself, at any site, seemed no closer than it had been 30 years before. Anyone expecting that to change may properly be classified an optimist.

Dedication of the new Mackinac Island marina, summer 1965. I was asked as Chamber manager to be emcee. Also on the platform and playing larger roles were Waterways Commission chairman Leonard Thomson (center right). Seated next to him, Governor and Mrs. George Romney. Brian Dunnigan, a summer resident who would go on to a distinguished career as a professional historian, is in costume at left under the American flag.

Funding the Park: Budget Battles

Finding enough money to run the Mackinac Island State Park has always been a major on-going challenge for the Commission. Probably no other issue commanded more of my time and ingenuity as Chair of that body, yet most of the work was behind the scenes and in the Lansing state capitol arena.

Monies for the Park have always come from two major sources: (1) admissions, rents, and fees, and (2) appropriations by the State Legislature from the general fund, the State's "catch all" repository of non-earmarked tax revenue. During the Blanchard Administration the Commission's ability to garner substantial general fund appropriations was enhanced by its hiring, at the behest of House Appropriations chairman Dominic Jacobetti, former State Senator Stanley "Stash" Novak to be its paid lobbyist. It was an uncomfortable move in some respects, however, because Novak was being compensated to advocate for things not necessarily consistent with the legislative goals of the Department (Natural Resources) to which the Commission was technically attached.

Novak, a kindly man not known for his intellectual prowess, had first become acquainted with Mackinac from his days as a member of the Senate Commerce Committee when he tended to the Island House liquor license and enjoyed that hotel's largesse. Novak, however, was effective on the Commission's behalf precisely because of his close relationship with his patron, the powerful "Godfather of Appropriations." When I became Commission chairman in February 1991, one of my first phone calls was from Jacobetti asking me to keep Novak on the Commission payroll. I agreed but was relieved when not long afterward Novak decided to retire coincident with Jacobetti's fall from political grace following a scandal involving key members of his legislative staff.

Even with Stash Novak's departure, the Commission fared well in appropriations matters. Governor Engler liked Mackinac Island, and my strong relationship with leaders of his Administration didn't hurt either. In 2002, the last year of the Engler budgets, the State's general fund appropriation to the Park peaked at $2 million. Admissions, rents, fees, and other assorted revenues boosted our overall revenues for operations to several millions more.

Once again, however, the media spotted what they believed to be a "hot story" and the July 2, 1994, *Detroit Free Press* featured a front page banner story, "Mackinac Parks Feast While Others Starve." Saying the Commission's overall budget had grown from $2.5 million to $5 million over the space of a few years, the article quoted a critic who claimed the additional money had "gone largely for an inflated staff, costly promotion, and costumed play-acting that haven't boosted attendance and trivialize important historic sites." The critic, it turned out, was a disaffected staff archaeologist who thought (surprise!) the Commission should have spent more money digging up artifacts on Fort grounds. Tom Washington couldn't resist leaping into the media fray and reiterated his belief that the Commission should be abolished and the Park treated like "the other state parks." The *Free Press* article went on to say that "Mackinac Island and the forts are coddled jewels" and that the Commission, "the prize plum among the hundreds of political appointments a Michigan governor can make," operates with "remarkable autonomy."

My response was that the Commission believed it necessary to "enliven" its presentation of history and to "put emphasis on colorful personnel and displays" while remaining "true to our historical mission." As for attendance, it indeed was flat, but so was traffic to the Island, and we shined by comparison to historical sites across the nation nearly all of which were experiencing declining attendance. The *Free Press*-induced crisis passed and the rest of the 1990s were good years for state appropriations for both park operations and capital outlay. One highlight was a $4.5 million restoration of Fort Mackinac's 1780 stone walls completed in 2001-2002.

The good times came to an abrupt end in 2003. The State's fiscal situation had deteriorated significantly, and the Commission's general fund budget was cut nearly ten percent. Then in 2005 Governor Jennifer Granholm was convinced by her director of the Department of Natural Resources to take an entirely new tack in funding Mackinac Island. Her plan called for the Park's general fund appropriation going from $1.5 million, to which by now it had sunk, to zero funding. Unveiling her budget, the Governor called for the Commission to replace all general funds with money from unspecified sources. Her remarks suggested that she favored an entry fee for persons setting foot on the Island. When asked by the press, I responded that her proposal was "just not workable" because there are 20 points of entry from the City to the Park and the Commission had no authority – absent legislation signed by the governor—to impose a tax on boat passengers arriving at the docks located in the City.

The Governor's proposal, however unworkable, posed a major dilemma for me and other members of the Commission. On the one hand, as Commissioners we were technically – and practically – members of the Governor's Administration. It was therefore touchy, if not unseemly, for Commissioners to outright oppose "our" Governor's policy initiative. On the other hand, we knew the idea of an entry fee could not possibly fly, legally or politically, and without adequate revenues the crown jewel of Michigan we had taken an oath to protect would be irreparably harmed.

A downstate newspaper envisions Mackinac Island's future after Gov. Granholm announces a budget that would eliminate state funding for the Park, 2005.

In response, I came up with a two-pronged strategy and prayed it would work. The first step was to create three Commission task forces that would seek additional and alternative sources of funding: one to look at private monies from foundations, another to look at new or increased user fees, and the last to check out possible federal funds. The last two were the most critical, and here the statutory requirement of Commission bi-partisanship came in very handy. With Commissioners Kelley and Traxler, prominent Democrats, heading these task forces the Governor would be hard-pressed to ascribe a partisan political motive or to deny the legitimacy of their findings. The task forces labored diligently and sincerely, and the conclusion they reached was pretty much as we knew it would be: there would be a yawning gap between what we could raise from new sources and what we would lose from zero general fund monies. In short, the Granholm plan simply would not work.

The second step in our response to the Governor's proposal was to quietly encourage formation of a grassroots citizens group that would work to rally public opposition to the Governor's proposal. Again, it was a fine line to be trod, but I encouraged the heads of five young families who were Mackinac devotees to organize "Families United for Mackinac" (FUND-MAC). Led by Brad Conkey of Sylvan Lake and Mike Gidley of Farmington Hills, the group held a press conference, wrote letters to the editor, contacted state legislators, and did many other things that would have been awkward for Commissioners themselves to do as members of the Granholm Administration.

The two-pronged strategy worked. The Governor soon distanced herself from the entry fee idea, legislators scrambled to support us, and the media also swung in our favor. To satisfy the Governor, many user fees were raised and new multiple sources of revenue were identified by the Commission. But in the end the legislature, with a bill signed by the governor, restored our $1.5 million in general funds. Helping our cause was a public hearing the House of Representatives held on the governor's original proposal. Chaired by an avowed Mackinac supporter, Rep. Fran Amos of Oakland County, the committee heard a deluge of testimony in opposition to the Governor, with the Commission essentially sitting as side-line observers and avoiding any direct action that would embarrass the governor. When the legislative hearing concluded, the budget battle of 2005 was no longer in doubt.

Funding concerns, however, did not go away in the years after 2005. Each subsequent year I worked with legislators in a low-key way to increase the Commission's general fund monies and was generally successful. In 2011 there came an unexpected development. The Commission was back within the Department of Natural Resources for budgeting purposes and the DNR director in the new Snyder Administration came to me with a proposal. The general fund outlook, he said, continued to be unstable and under continuing pressure. Would we consider giving up general fund appropriations in exchange for a guaranteed base level of money coming from the State Park Endowment Fund with an additional guarantee of future increases at least as large in percentage as increases going to other state parks? For many of the reasons outlined by DNR Director Rod Stokes we agreed to his proposal and in the first year of the new regimen, Fiscal Year 2011-12, we received $1.6 million, slightly more than we would likely have gotten from a general fund appropriation.

The following year, the House and Senate chairs of the DNR appropriations subcommittees both expressed to me their interest in doing "more" for Mackinac Island. I told them the Commission itself was bound by our agreement with the DNR but if they, as legislative appropriations chairs, wanted to do something additional, that was their business. Accordingly, in the FY 2012-13 budget, an additional $275,000 above the earlier base of $1.6 million was added and our grand total of state aid at last began to approach the $2 million we were appropriated back in 2002. When adding the increased and new fees resulting from the 2005 Granholm proposal, our total revenues now stood at $7.2 million, less than the optimum, but still far better than would otherwise have been the case.

With the help of a lot of people, we were able to surmount the fiscal crisis of our darkest days. I have no doubt, however, that securing adequate funding will continue to be a major Commission challenge well into the future.

St. Ignace Mayor Bruce Dodson (L) cements the connection between the two communities by greeting Islander Calvin "Cubby" Horn and Mayor Margaret Doud upon their arrival on the traditional "first boat of the season," April 2005.

Mid-1970s Police Chief Otto Wandrie, when he wasn't firing shots to break up the antics of St. Ignace visitors, cut an imposing figure on horseback. Even Islander Stanley Green, on bicycle, seems to do a double-take. Wandrie, whose paternal grandparents and cousins operated an Island restaurant until the early 1960s, was the last Island police officer to patrol on horseback.

The St. Ignace Connection

Many people, viewing the matter from afar, assume that if the Mackinac Island community has a bond with any mainland community it must be with Mackinaw City, across the Straits and situated at the top of the lower peninsula.

It is with the people and the community of St. Ignace, however, that Mackinac Islanders have traditionally identified and bonded, almost to the exclusion of Mackinaw City. By water, St. Ignace is geographically closer, and in the long months of winter the ice bridge between the Island and that town has forged a link and an interdependence between the two. Many Islanders, particularly ones of French-Indian extraction, have extended families in St. Ignace and some Islanders even "retire to" St. Ignace. The fact that the town is also the county seat and the site of the county's only funeral home only strengthens the cross-water ties. When St. Ignace school teams do well in state sports tournaments, as they often do, perhaps their biggest fans can be found on Mackinac Island. It was one of my regrets as a State Park Commissioner that sufficient funds was never available, at least in my time, to operate an appropriate historic facility in St. Ignace, a town that dates its settlement back to the 17th century.

Even a St. Ignace "invasion" in June 1973 did nothing to fray traditional ties. The two communities made headlines in the *Detroit Free Press* for what the paper then described as an event that was "sure to be the Upper Peninsula's best-remembered bachelor party." Seven St. Ignace men – including the mayor and two high school coaches – were charged with a total of 18 misdemeanors after a high-speed midnight boat ride to the Island to finish out a riotous evening that began on the mainland. In the process, one Island policeman was knocked unconscious, and a bar emptied in pandemonium. Police Chief Otto Wandrie, arriving late to the scene by bicycle, fired his service pistol to get the brawling crowd's attention and even then had trouble restoring order.

The event is still remembered by some—with ever expanding details—as a classic story of Mackinac's "good old days."

Nurse King's Dream

Mackinac Island's Medical Center over the years has been a true "life line" of the community. Dating back before my time, Island doctors and dentists operated out of their own small, cramped offices. Following World War II, the flood of tourists made it evident that a modern complete medical center was sorely needed.

The Island's public health nurse, stoic, poker-faced Stella King, a life-long resident, was particularly aware of the need. Miss King had seen countless local residents through trying times and watched in frustration as five or more doctors left their Island practice because of the outdated and inadequate facilities available to them. All too frequently Miss King was the community's sole source of medical services. Aided and encouraged by four enterprising local women who undertook fund-raising bake sales, Nurse King led the effort to build a new facility. It opened in 1954, thanks to prodigious local efforts, and was licensed as a one-bed maternity hospital.

During the 1970s, particularly, Mayor Doud worked assiduously to keep the Medical Center financially afloat. An affiliation was entered into with William Beaumont Hospital and still later with a rejuvenated Mackinac Straits Hospital with Rod Nelson as administrator.

In 2004 Nelson asked if there was anything I could do to help the Medical Center obtain from the federal government an "emergency room" designation for cost reimbursement purposes. Inquiring of the Michigan Department of Public Health, I was told I was on an impossible mission and basically urged not to waste my time. Fortunately, I had some excellent contacts within the very top echelons of the U.S. Department of Health and Human Services, and I pled the Island's case. As a result, Mackinac Island became one of the very few non-hospital facilities in the entire country to gain ER status, and it brought the Medical Center several hundred thousands of dollars annually in new insurance reimbursements. It was a desperately needed financial shot-in-the-arm at a critical moment.

In addition, largely as a result of good relations Islanders built at the annual Friends of Mackinac event in Lansing, key legislators and State Public Health Director Jim Haveman came through with generous assistance to build in 2006 a much larger, state-of-the-art Medical Center. Health services had indeed come a long way from the days of Nurse King and the ladies' bake sales.

Dock Porters

Best job on the Island? Many locals will tell you it's dock porter, those lithe young men (and the occasional woman) who greet incoming visitors on the Island's three passenger docks, sort, collect, and tag luggage, and then pedal huge loads of it by bike to the Island's hotels and guest houses.

"Dock porter is the job every guy wants. Chicks dig dock porters," says one Islander. And, making $600 to as much as $800 a week in tips isn't bad duty either, though it can be persuasively argued they earn every penny of it.

Visitors to Mackinac are often awe-struck by the athletic grace and foolhardy courage that it takes to put up to 400 pounds in and atop a basket moving on two wheels and maneuvered from a high seat through a street awash in pedestrians and horse-drawn vehicles.

"Riding the perfect load becomes a holy quest," one dock porter told David McVeigh for a 1991 article in *The Chicago Tribune*. Careful planning, consideration of the laws of gravity, and a special bravado are also essential. Timing a load's arrival at a guest's hotel is also important since a visual of a skilled,

Loaded for action, dock porter Robert Chambers.

Josh Carley prepares for take-off.

acrobatic dock porter can produce heightened customer appreciation (read: enhanced gratuities).

Meeting six boats an hour from 8 a.m. to 8 p.m., each loaded with passengers and luggage is not for the faint of heart. Mild chaos in the baggage area is the norm. Fortunately, dock porters know that teamwork is essential and, even though their employers may be business rivals, a fraternity-like camaraderie among the porters themselves develops early in the season.

For many years, the Dock Porter's Ball was a major season-ending social event for the college worker crowd, and an invitation to it much coveted among the Island's co-ed workers.

Proof of the job's desirability is the fact that most "baggage smashers" come back for several seasons. The record for dock porter longevity is held by Glen Woulfe who retired in 2013 from Windermere Hotel after 29 years of service.

Dan Dewey hauls a load in the 1970s.

The Convention and Visitors Bureau: Adequate Funding At Last

Toward the end of my tenure as Chamber of Commerce Manager back in 1965, a friend said I had done a good job in laying a foundation for the Chamber's future and that undoubtedly, in the years to come, its facilities and funding would only get better.

For the most part, they didn't. Nearly fifty years later, the offices of the Chamber (now called the Tourism Bureau) are as tiny, cramped, and inadequate as ever. Its budget didn't improve much either. Despite an energetic and talented manager, the Bureau's paid advertising was practically non-existent. Island promotion was, in a word, "bush league" and this at a time when competing destinations were pouring literally millions of dollars into paid advertising. The source of their funds was a locally imposed tax on hotel rooms. By state law, however, Mackinac Island was barred from using this revenue source.

In December 2009, I invited Dan Musser, Grand Hotel's owner and chairman of its board, to lunch and told him I thought it was time for Island business leaders to re-evaluate their position and seek a change in state law. A few days later, Musser called me back to say Grand Hotel was "on board." The dream of my Chamber years, finances and facilities worthy of a world-class destination seemed, after nearly a half century, to be at last in sight.

Now the task would be to convince the legislature to change the law and let Mackinac Island do what virtually every other municipality in the state could do: levy a tax on rooms to fund a Convention and Visitors Bureau that would aggressively promote visits to and overnight stays on the Island. On the surface, getting a legislative re-write should not have been difficult, especially for one such as I who had devoted much of my legal practice to doing that very thing for clients that ranged from Ford Motor Company to American Express. It turned out to be not so simple. Senate Republicans viewed the bill I drafted as being a "tax increase," passage of which would be contrary to their publicly stated position. I eventually convinced Republican leadership to let the bill come to a vote, then persuaded a bare majority of senators that it was not a tax but rather the option of allowing a voluntary private assessment. The bill passed.

    The battle shifted to the House of Representatives. There the Democratic Speaker vowed to kill the bill because its sponsor was a Republican Senator, Jason Allen, who would be running for U.S. Congress in the fall against a member of his House Democratic caucus. (In the contorted view of politicians, passage of a bill – any bill – gives the sponsor bragging rights and a perceived political leg up.) My task thus became one of convincing the Speaker that it would be political suicide for his candidate, State Rep. Gary McDowell, to be seen as blocking a bill of great importance to Mackinac Island. The Speaker relented. The bill passed the House, was signed by the Governor, and became law on May 21, 2010. Ironically, neither Senator Allen nor Representative McDowell was elected to Congress that fall. Allen was upset in the Republican primary, and the man who defeated him by 14 votes, Dr. Dan Benishek, went on to defeat McDowell in the November general election.

    Shortly thereafter, hotel owners on the Island approved the assessment allowed by the revised state law. I drew up incorporation papers for the new Mackinac Island Convention and Visitors Bureau, and by summer we were levying the new 2% room tax. Within a year the Island had at its disposal nearly a million dollars in new advertising money, and its value in generating business soon became apparent.

Bob Benser Jr. of the Chippewa and Lilac Tree Hotels and Dan Musser III of Grand Hotel, roommates at Albion College, my undergraduate alma mater, were early leaders of the new Mackinac Island Convention and Visitors Bureau. Todd Callewaert of Island House also played a key role. State legislation I drafted and advocated for made its creation and funding possible, but not before some typical Lansing political infighting over its enactment.

The Chamber of Commerce (later Tourism Bureau) office, shown here in winter 1966, remained cramped and dysfunctional for nearly another half century despite the huge importance of tourism to the Island.

The Great Ferry Wars of 2010-2014

The Great Ferry Wars of 2010-2014 marked one of the most fractious and controversial events of my first 54 years on Mackinac. It received extensive, on-going coverage in the downstate media. Its causes and the true facts surrounding it need telling, simply because so much about it has been distorted or misunderstood.

When I first came to Mackinac one boat line was dominant. That was Arnold Transit Company, founded in 1878 and historically the only full-season provider of both freight and passenger service. Since the depths of the Depression it had been owned by the Prentiss Brown family who had purchased it from the estate of Susan Arnold, widow of an original State Park Commission member, Island resident George Arnold. In 1960 it had one out-gunned competitor, Straits Transit Company, which operated only out of Mackinaw City and was owned by former state car ferry employees based in Cheboygan. When they lost their jobs because of the Mackinac Bridge, the workers took over a small existing ferry company and purchased one of the now out-of-service state car ferries, the Straits of Mackinac.

The ship was a paradox. It had a capacity of 1,000 passengers and made the trip from Mackinaw City to Mackinac Island in just over 45 minutes. When it was in port at the Mackinaw City docks it was, in the words of one observer, "like a vacuum cleaner." Its impressive size, huge smoke-billowing stacks, and gleaming white structure, sucked up every would-be passenger desiring water passage to the Island. Its Achilles' heel, however, was its very size and cost of operations. Ultimately, the ship proved not economically viable. It was finally sold sometime in the late-1960s and Straits Transit was left to rely on a tiny fleet of old, small diesel-powered vessels operating out of a single mainland port. Arnold tried to deliver a death blow to its weakened competitor by seeking to buy controlling shares in Straits Transit. I remember my astonishment when, one day at Harvard Law, my corporations professor directed us to analyze the Michigan Supreme Court decision in *Straits Transit v. Union Terminal Piers* (Arnold Transit) as an example of a hostile takeover.

Operating also out of Mackinaw City, but only as a special charter service, was a tiny company called Shepler's. In the 1970s Shepler's expanded into a full service line and soon acquired a sterling reputation for its fast, quality service and immaculate vessels. Eventually it expanded into St. Ignace. Also in the 1970s, fudge mogul Harry Ryba briefly got into the freight and passenger boat business. Still another small boat line, the Argosy, operated only out of St. Ignace, and in 1977 it was acquired by a group of locals led by Tom Pfeiffelman and renamed Star Line. In the mid-1970s Arnold finally succeeded in swallowing Straits Transit, and the latter company soon passed from the scene. A decade later, Arnold Transit, tired of being compared to Shepler's clean, fast boats, finally transitioned to a fleet of even faster catamarans. It did, however, continue to operate one boat from the old fleet, the Huron, which was better suited for navigating the ice clogging the Straits in winter.

By the mid-2000s, however, all three operating lines were faced with the economic reality of competing in a shrinking market. Traffic to the Island had fallen from a high of nearly 900,000 in 2000 to less than 750,000 in 2011. Many vessels often operated nearly empty, their owners fearing to drop trips, however unprofitable, lest the competition run a full schedule and get a leg up. Moreover, the fleets of all three were getting tired and fuel prices had gone through the roof. Plainly, the system taken as whole was grossly inefficient.

As far back as the mid-1970s, the City of Mackinac Island decided it needed to get a much better handle on the ferries while at the same time picking up additional revenue for local government coffers. It imposed a 25 cents tax on each boat ticket. Arnold Line, in particular, protested and took a legal challenge all the way to the Michigan Supreme Court. When the Court refused to hear a lower court decision in favor of the City, the tax was cemented in place. The Booth newspapers, operating seven major Michigan dailies, reported on the situation:

> "For politics per square inch, there is no place in Michigan—not even the state capital—that can match Mackinac Island. That blue-green emerald island in the Straits of Mackinac has a lusty history of brawling, rough-and-tumble politics . . . The one major ferry service (read Arnold Line) that carries 95% of the passengers from St. Ignace and 60% from Mackinaw City – might decide to withhold service. The fear of economic strangulation had the Mackinac Island City Council scrambling to adopt an ordinance that would regulate the ferry service . . . for the first time in 78 years . . . The fear is that Arnold Line is moving toward monopolistic control of the island . . . Rumors (to that effect) got around the Island faster than a ten speed bike."

A good part of the City's anxiety was fueled by concerns raised by the Lansing law firm it hired to defend the boat passenger tax. The City's regular attorney was Prentiss Brown Jr., but since his family's company was the chief target of the new tax, it opted for outside counsel. Spotting what it correctly perceived was a huge vulnerability in the City's bargaining power, the new lawyers pressed for greater ferry regulation and for the City to acquire ownership of one or more docks. The City council subsequently forged ahead with a set of loose regulations, but the costly acquisition of docks was left for a later day.

City taxation and regulation of the boats reposed in quietude for the next quarter century and more. It was all about to change. In addition to escalating costs, declining revenues, and a litany of inefficiencies in common with the other two companies, Arnold was facing an intra-family crisis. The descendants of Prentiss M. Brown, Sr. were numerous, and ownership of Arnold was now spread across many families. (Old "P.M" had five children and one of them had eleven children). Chafing under years of no dividends from their Arnold stock and seeing the passage of the older generation of Browns, some in the family signaled their willingness to sell to outsiders. That touched off a major internal struggle that bitterly split those who wanted ownership to remain within the family, perhaps in concert with outsiders if necessary, against those family members who just wanted "out."

At about the same time Jim Wynn, a Petoskey attorney who specialized in business affairs, was hired by one of the boat lines to study operations and make recommendations for efficiencies. What he saw convinced him that the lines could become profitable – perhaps wildly so – if they would just consolidate into one company. Learning that a narrow majority of the Browns were now ready to sell he set about to acquire Arnold and consolidate the three boat lines with himself as owner of the new mega-company. Star Line, the smallest of the three but a plucky competitor, clearly favored consolidation. A preliminary agreement was reached whereby Shepler, too, would essentially sell out to the man who had originally been their attorney/analyst. The only missing piece was final victory by the pro-sale elements of the Brown family. The latter eventually won out and the Petoskey attorney signed final purchase papers in early summer of 2010, believing that he was on the brink of unifying the three companies under his ownership.

In the meantime, however, the Shepler interests had a change of heart. Not only were any preliminary agreements for consolidation out the window, but Shepler correctly divined that it needed to ratchet up its competitive efforts. Star Line, however, agreed to enter into a new operating alliance with Arnold, in an effort by both to achieve at least minimal operating efficiencies. Complicating matters for Arnold's new owners was the fact that on the very day of its purchase, Grand Hotel decided to pull its "preferred carrier" status from

Quieter days for Island ferries. In 1962, as Chamber manager I chatted aside the Arnold Line's Ottawa with Hugh Rudolph, assistant general manager, and his wife Mariana (Nan) Rudolph, daughter of company co-owner Prentiss M. Brown. In those days Arnold, led by general manager and co-owner Otto Lang, was by far the dominant carrier.

Arnold and hand it to a highly appreciative Shepler. Suddenly, the early assumptions of Arnold's new owners were no longer valid.

The latest gyrations, however, did not go unnoticed by the City of Mackinac Island and its lawyers. Seeing the renewed possibility of monopoly, the City's reaction this time around was very different than it was in the 1970s, and with good reason. With proper regulation, a monopoly now could finally achieve the kind of efficiencies that might force ticket prices down and the number of customers sharply up. In short, many now saw monopoly as potentially a good thing. Further, the new Arnold owner, saddled with huge debt, signaled a desire to sell to the City and then lease back its Island dock and storage facilities, potentially a huge win for both parties.

The root of Shepler's concern, now that it had opted out of a voluntary merger, was that the City might grant Arnold an exclusive franchise that would essentially put Shepler's out of business. In other words, though the merger was off, the idea of merger-like efficiencies were not, in the City's mind. The possible sale of an Arnold dock to the City also loomed large in Bill Shepler's thinking. All of this was fueled by the memory of his past battles with the City of Mackinac Island. There was an awareness that Arnold had always been regarded by Islanders as their "home town" boat line and Shepler an opportunistic outsider. Visions of a City-Arnold conspiracy were not far from Shepler's thoughts and on the surface there appeared some justification.

Even before this development, the owners of at least two of the boat lines (and possibly the third, I can't recall) approached me and our law firm about the possibility of providing them with governmental affairs advice and counsel, the thought apparently being that our help might be essential in case either the legislature or state regulators might seek to block or at least modify any merger or monopoly. When Shepler fell out of the would-be merger, the new owner of Arnold, on the very day he concluded his purchase, contacted me to say he wanted to hire our firm for governmental affairs consulting. Since the State Park Commission, unlike the City, had absolutely no regulatory or other role in ferry matters, I saw no conflict of interest. After consulting my partner Frank Kelley we took on the task. When, in time, the renewed Arnold-Shepler rivalry resumed, Bill Shepler contacted me to inquire if I would represent him and I had to explain to him that we were, regretfully, already engaged.

The fur soon began to fly. Shepler hired a Lansing lobbying firm and a very good public relations firm to tell its story and put the City and Arnold on the defensive. Arnold retaliated by asking us to recommend, in addition to ourselves, still another lobbying firm and a PR firm. Within a short time, Shepler-inspired legislation was introduced in Lansing to wipe out all or part of the City's state-granted charter, long jealously guarded by its local government. Instead, under the proposed bill, the state would control ferry operations. The City, at my recommendation, also hired its own lobbying firm to do battle in Lansing. Meantime, the PR firms fired blazing guns at one another, with many of the Shepler bombs being lobbed at the Mayor and City Council. Our lobbying team prevailed, however, and the Shepler-inspired bill died, if for no other reason than the Legislature ran out of time to consider it before adjournment of the 2010 session.

Early 2011 was dominated by lawsuits filed between the contending parties in state and federal courts. Initially foregoing a renewed legislative effort, Shepler turned its attention to the State Public Service Commission. That Commission's jurisdiction was at least somewhat sketchy, but it pressed ahead with plans to hold public hearings on the whole controversy that promised to give the City and probably Arnold a black eye. None of it was good for the Island's tourism industry. Mr. Kelley and I worked hard to convince the Public Service Commission it should stay out of what we described as essentially a local fight, albeit of epic proportions. This time we again prevailed, but there was no question that on the PR front -- largely out of our control --Shepler was winning big time in the court of public opinion. Meantime, the various lawsuits between the parties were dismissed or otherwise bogged down.

The City Council, weary and seeking some measure of temporary peace, voted to grant short-term franchises to all three companies. Any thought of a single franchise and monopoly was essentially dead. New franchise fees were set at 7% of ticket revenues, which some suspected was designed to push Shepler's precarious financial situation over the edge. At 7%, the tax now amounted to approximately $1.50 per ticket, six times the original tax. In addition, the City placed heavy regulation on schedules and other details of operations.

The resulting peace was too good to last, however. Upset on a number of fronts, Shepler renewed its fight in Lansing in early 2012 with the introduction of new legislation aimed at the City. The company found a willing bill sponsor who, having ridden a boat several times in high season to Mackinac Island, thought that he "knew" all about the issue. What he and others failed to understand was that the City's concern was not so much summertime passenger service but freight and winter time runs that, if abandoned by the only company that had ever provided it, would perhaps leave the local community totally isolated. Meantime, for a number of reasons, our firm in late January 2012 chose to resign from our representation of Union Terminal Piers. The City, now facing a Lansing battle alone, hired back its old lobbying firm and directed it to stop the latest legislative assault.

By May 2012, a number of Island leaders, myself included, were increasingly concerned with the unending, hair-pulling battle that was beginning to seriously tarnish the Island's reputation. A decision was made that, given all the economic and political clout at our disposal, five of us should insist that representatives of the City and the three boat lines meet behind locked doors and emerge only when all parties had signed a compromise agreement that would put the entire matter to bed for the foreseeable future. Thus Dan Musser Jr., Dan Musser III of Grand Hotel, Bill Chambers and Brad Chambers of Carriage Tours, Inc., and myself, representing I'm not quite sure who, summoned the warring parties to the Grand Hotel on a Saturday morning in late July.

After meeting all that day and a good part of Sunday a compromise agreement was finally reached: the boat tax was slashed from the old 7% of revenues level to a flat $600,000

a year, adjusted for inflation going forward and split equally between the three companies; guaranteed winter service was subsidized; operational rules were loosened; state legislation affecting the City's charter withdrawn. At a packed house public meeting in the Community Hall several days later I took the lead in describing the package to a skeptical audience. Messrs. Mussers and Chambers provided valuable back-up support. The audience reaction was generally favorable, to our considerable relief.

The next step was consideration of our compromise package by the City Council. As we expected, adoption did not come easily. Several times a supportive Mayor Margaret Doud seemed ready to throw in the towel, and two of the boat companies threatened to withdraw their earlier endorsement. In the end, Council was convinced to adopt the agreement and its implementing ordinance. Not unexpectedly, the vote was not unanimous.

It would be nice to say that everyone lived happily ever after. The truth is otherwise. Arnold, subject of over a dozen lawsuits for breach of various contracts with vendors, continued to struggle and squandered nearly all of the local goodwill the company had built up over its previous 136 years of operation. Star Line ended its operating agreement with Arnold on a contentious note and its able general manager, Tom Pfeiffelman, retired from the company. Arnold Line still faced continuing economic pressures. By early 2014, final outcome of the Great Ferry Wars remained in doubt, though Shepler and Star, once "little brothers" to Arnold, appeared best positioned to survive going forward.

A lone generator-powered light illuminates the southwest end of downtown at the height of the black-out crisis.

Blackout 2000

One of the most bizarre incidents in the Island's recent history occurred over eleven days at the very peak of the 2000 summer tourism season. From Saturday, July 22 to early Wednesday, August 2 the Island endured sustained power outages that shut down cooking and cooling equipment at every Mackinac bar, restaurant, hotel, and home and plunged the town into total darkness for most of every night.

Cause of the disaster was failure of six of the seven submarine cables that carry power under the Straits of Mackinac to the Island's west side. The cables, heavily insulated with steel jackets designed for service in Norway's fjords, were apparently incapable of dissipating their heat when buried and the result was a "cooking" that triggered cascading breaks.

For the first four days, the power interruptions were long but intermittent. Each day officials of Edison Sault Electric, the Island's power provider, issued optimistic statements that the power would be permanently on by that night. Each night it wasn't. "The emotional roller coaster of all this is one of the hardest things to cope with. It's on, off, up, down," shop owner Peter Marabell told the *Detroit Free Press*.

During those first days of the crisis hotels operated on candlelight, lanterns, or small generators while restaurants and bars cooked meals on charcoal and gas grills and relied on ice trucked and barged from the mainland. All of this during the always hectic two weeks of the Chicago to Mackinac and Bay View to Mackinac yacht races.

When on the fifth day there occurred a fire at the point where the cables come on to Mackinac's shore, the power shut down completely. Frustrated and angry, the community demanded action. Under pressure, Edison Sault Electric agreed to absorb the cost of six mammoth diesel-powered generators being shipped to the Island from as far away as Pennsylvania. Meantime, a midnight curfew was declared and tall, temporary banks of generator-powered lights provided the downtown with a surreal illumination.

Despite the calamity, tourists, businesses, and townspeople handled the matter with relative aplomb. Tourist traffic was down only marginally, the hotels nearly fully occupied.

Some visitors actually thought it was "fun," evocative of Victorian times. Hamburgers and hotdogs, plus the occasional steak and even a wedding cake, were prepared on grills, and diners were happy to have what they could get. A flourishing business in T-shirts, "I Survived Blackout 2000 on Mackinac," soon took off, and the Island received nation-wide coverage in a demonstration of "any publicity is good publicity."

When the power went on to stay at 5 a.m. August 2, the Island breathed a huge collective sigh of relief. Many were just thankful that the blackout, bad as it was, occurred in summer. Said Mayor Doud, "If this had happened in the winter (when every home and business is heated by electricity) the Island would have had to be evacuated."

Even cartoonists couldn't resist a wry chuckle at Mackinac's blackout debacle in this reference to the popular TV show "Survivor."

"The Voice of Mackinac Island"

That's the appellation fondly accorded Jeannette Doud who for the last three decades of my 54 years on the Island has chronicled life and times for the local *Town Crier* and the *St. Ignace News*.

"Every week, readers eagerly comb through her column, searching for news of long-time friends, weddings, births, and deaths. The column helps them visualize their Island when they can't be there. Her writing … is … a loving look at what is going on through her Island-tinted glasses," observed the magazine *Mackinac Living*.

Says Wes Mauer Jr., publisher of the two newspapers, "She sings her song and is joyful about the things she writes and is sad when sad things happen … She doesn't think of (her long and richly detailed columns) as a drudgery but as a social obligation and a commitment … I love reading her column, too."

Born on the Island over nine decades ago, she married the mayor of the Island, Robert Doud, when she was nineteen years old. After World War II the couple began helping to operate the Windermere Hotel and in time became the owners. Family pride swelled when their only child, Margaret, became mayor in 1975, the first female to hold the office and by 2014 the longest continuously serving mayor in the state of Michigan.

In my earlier times on the Island, from 1960 to the 1980s, other reporters ably filled local news columns with colorful accounts of local happenings, including Lenore Goodheart, Catherine Doyle, and Lorabeth Fitzgerald. It is safe to say, however, that none could quite match the unique, insightful, exuberant style of Jeannette Doud.

A Place Like No Other

I have often said that I would not trade our very modest cottage, nestled among towering pines on a secluded beach, for any mansion on the Island's east or west bluff.

It was built in the spring of 1973 when I was young, single, and impecunious. It has been added to over the years, reflecting my marital state, a growing family, and improved financial circumstances. What our home still lacks in size and amenities, it more than compensates in the wonder of its natural setting.

I had picked out this stretch of beach as my favorite on the Island during one of my first summers. That I would end up owning it through sheer good fortune, and then building my home upon it, I always regarded as something of a miracle. The cedar-sided cottage lies in a natural clearing hemmed in by tall conifers. Only a single tree was felled to make room for the structure. Today it is the only home on the Island, outside of downtown and the boardwalk area, situated directly on the beach between the shore road and the waters of Lake Huron.

The cottage sits just fifty feet from Lake Huron's edge. Mackinac is not noted for its fine beaches but ours is probably the best that can be found on the Island. In the rare summer that is hot enough, we occasionally venture into a lake that struggles to reach 70 degrees and drops off to great depths just yards offshore.

In late spring and early summer nearby bluffs protect us from the damp, cool east winds that often mar that season for the rest of the Island. We face due west, three miles of clean deep water separating us from St. Ignace and Michigan's Upper Peninsula. From our shore, it is possible with one sweep of the eye to see from south to north an expanse of nearly 20 miles, beginning just below the Mackinac Bridge then to well beyond St. Ignace where the Upper Peninsula juts to the east.

At dusk we marvel at spectacular sunsets straight ahead and in late summer a golden full moon sets over St. Ignace just before daybreak. At night the sky is alive with countless bright stars. The Milky Way stretches over us in a high arc north north-east to south south-west. Northern lights, even in the summer, are not uncommon. Neither are lightning-charged storms that start to cross the lake, then often split and miss the Island by going north and south.

By day, from the all-glass front of our cottage we see water meeting sky in an infinite number of variations: the changing angle of the sun as days and seasons progress; the direction of the water, its constant reconfiguration from glassy surface to ripples to gently rolling swells to thunderous pounding waves; the shifting arrangement and density of clouds. All of these create a moving tableaux of color, light, and texture that no artist could ever replicate on canvas.

When our family seeks some simple diversion, we take our coffee to the cottage's back deck. There, less than 20 feet from the shore road that encircles the island, but hidden by a thick growth of pines, we can hear the conversation and chatter of the hundreds of bicyclists who pass by every hour and yet who do not see us. Tiring of that, and as the morning sun climbs higher into the southern and western sky, we move around to the front deck of the cottage for the quiet and solitude of a sun-filled beach and views of far-off sailboats, ferries, and freighters.

In the night, from the open windows of our bedrooms, no sound is heard save the sound of Lake Huron's waters lapping, sometimes pounding the shore just 50 feet away, pines rustling gently overhead, seagulls crying in the far distance. This is our home.

Changing Times

Time and the pace of life does move more slowly on Mackinac than it does almost any other place in America. Its Victorian style of architecture, its horses, buggies, and bicycles are all remnants of a time gone by. Mackinac loves its past and yields only grudgingly to change in any form. The "good old days" are fondly remembered. Yet the fact is that change has come to Mackinac in the half century since I arrived. Most of it has been good, some of it not so good.

In January 2013, after long consideration and debate, the City Council approved the creation of two downtown historic districts. Going forward, demolition of historic buildings would be prohibited and renovation of existing buildings must meet standards established for historic structures by the U.S. Secretary of the Interior. The Mackinac Island State Park Commission had adopted these standards for homes and other buildings under its jurisdiction back in 1992 at the time of the Great Lease Wars, and I was pleased we did. Along with several other downtown business owners I had been concerned at first that the proposed City districts did not have the support of affected owners that I believed was needed for successful implementation. However, when in late 2012 the owners of a number of downtown buildings started selling off their properties, I became very concerned about what could happen next. Approval of the downtown historic districts now clearly seemed the prudent course of action and it passed the City Council by a 5-1 vote in January 2013. Nancy May, Mac Trayser, and Lorna Straus were among the local citizens who pushed for historic district designations from the beginning. The battle over what should and could be allowed in the new historic districts raged on into 2014 with a final outcome yet to be determined.

In spite of it all, I believe that both the City and the Park look and feel far better today than they did fifty or twenty years ago. It bothered me greatly that writers of letters to the editor of the Island's *Town Crier* frequently lamented that Mackinac was losing its historic character and old-time magic. It seemed to me that anyone who has been on the Island for fifty or twenty years, if they had an accurate memory, would have to acknowledge that the general maintenance, condition, and appearance of the vast majority of downtown

Main Street as it appeared when I first arrived in 1960.

buildings is better now than it was in "the good old days." Of course there are exceptions, but I believe they are small in number. Sign control and the ban of "formula businesses," two things I fought hard to get enacted by the City, have also helped downtown's appearance and ambience.

A significant change, however, has occurred in Mackinac's residential areas. In 1960 and well into the early 1980s, Mackinac's neighborhoods were small in number and distinct in character: the East Bluff, West Bluff, and Annex for wealthy summer residents; Harrisonville, primarily for local residents of French-Indian descent; the Mission, Market Street, and the rest of the downtown area hugging the harbor, for all other year-round residents; and British Landing, for the owners of a small number of seasonal homes. Stonecliffe, Stonebrook, Sunset Forest, and Trillium Heights were neighborhoods far into the future, to be created on lands that in 1960 were thought to be unsuitable or impractical for development.

To no one did it occur that Harrisonville would also change significantly in the years that followed. In the 1980s, Island employers, reeling from the tragic LaSalle fire and its aftermath, looked for affordable land on which to build decent employee housing. Only Harrisonville offered the prospect of cheap land. Soon new housing sprouted up that brought itinerant workers into a neighborhood that was the historic home of about half the island's permanent residents. The incursion was not always welcomed. "Before they needed us for employee housing, they didn't want to be up here with us Indians; they didn't want to associate with us," one long-time Harrisonville resident told the *Detroit News* in 1996.

Soon Harrisonville land and old homes were selling for ten times their 1960 value. Many owners, suddenly rich beyond their wildest dreams, sold out and moved to the mainland, feeding the very trend they deplored. Today, Harrisonville is home to numerous employee housing complexes, but it is also true that its housing stock in general is far superior to what it had been in 1960. As for the permanent residents, they gained new pride when their tribe, the Sault Sainte Marie Tribe of Chippewa Indians, was accorded federal recognition sending social and economic benefits in the direction of the tribe's numerous Island members. The old, close-knit Harrisonville community of primarily French-Indian stock and very large families is now, too, pretty much just a memory.

Pollution issues have also been resolved, much for the better, in recent years. In 1990 the Clean Water Action, an environmental watchdog group, listed the City's sewage system in its "Filthy Five" list of Michigan polluters, and one of its spokesmen said, "Nobody else could get away with what the city of Mackinac Island gets away with" in dumping millions of gallons of poorly treated sewage into the Straits. City leaders responded by correctly pointing out the difficulty of a community of 450 persons paying for infrastructure used by 700,000 to 900,000 visitors annually. The problems were largely fixed a few years later, but the City still struggles with potential lack of capacity and keeping its sewage treatment plant up to code remains a constant challenge.

The array of Island business owners has also undergone change. When I first came, business owners fell into two categories: locals who just happened to be there when tourists pushed thru their doors seeking things the locals could furnish or sell and shrewd people from off the island who came to Mackinac knowing that their entrepreneurial skills would provide them a very good living. Harry Ryba was one of the latter, and he transformed the sleepy local fudge market by innovative and enterprising sales techniques, including wafting the delicious smell of cooking fudge out onto the street and into the nostrils of passing tourists.

Business ownership, or at least control of business real estate, is concentrated in fewer hands than ever. Grand Hotel has expanded its reach and the Chambers, Benser, Nephew, and Callewaert families have acquired in low key fashion many downtown properties. In contrast, one or two relative newcomers have also been aggressive in building, renovating, and marketing but in ways not always positive for the Island's over-all image. Their projects stirred bitter controversies that were still at a high boil in early 2014.

The Island's work force has also changed significantly. Where college students once dominated, by the late 1970s foreign students and seasonal workers with visas were in the majority. Several factors were responsible for the change. Colleges and universities changed their semester start and finish time. August departures became especially problematic for employers. A pronounced dis-inclination to work hard and appreciate the value of a dollar on the part of younger American workers caused many employers to look elsewhere for help. Foreigners, appreciative of their opportunities, filled the void. By the 1980s, workers came from the Caribbean and Mexico. After the fall of the Iron Curtain in 1990, workers and students came to Mackinac's shores from nearly all the old East Bloc countries. The Philippines and Canada also soon became major suppliers of labor.

Television, especially its presence in the bars, largely killed off the story-telling skills that locals honed in the early years. A few masters of the old genre remain. Dr. Bill Chambers and the much younger Jason St. Onge are capable of telling classic Mackinac stories in a way that rivals the great Mackinac tale-spinners of old.

Father Jim Williams has moved on, but during his active priesthood on the Island he left a mark with his enthusiasm, passion, and community outreach that went far across denominational lines. And the Island's *Town Crier* newspaper, often under-appreciated but

A new generation of Island leaders, 2013, each from families rooted deep in Mackinac's history. (L-R), Jason St. Onge, school board president, mayor pro-tem, assistant fire chief, and a card-carrying member of the Native American tribe that called Mackinac home; Sam Barnwell, city council member, whose grandfather served as mayor over a half century ago; Anneke Myers, city council member, whose father served for over a third of a century as deputy director and interim director of Mackinac State Historic Parks; and Andrew Doud, chair of the historic district commission, and owner of the nation's oldest independently owned grocery store, whose great-great-grandfather was an Irish immigrant settler of the Island over a century and a half ago.

perhaps one of the premier small town publications in the country, continues to play a key role informing and shaping the community. Its publisher, Wes Maurer Jr., like his father Wes Maurer Sr., consistently exhibits the highest standards of journalistic professionalism.

The Island school, which until the early 1960s, educated only thru the 10th grade, has also seen vast improvement. Today its course offerings, especially thru the Eastern Upper Peninsula Intermediate School District, rival that of most big city and suburban districts. A community foundation, where endowment is now over $6 million, assures that the Island has a source and safety net for expenditures benefiting the local population and local projects. These range from college scholarships to environmental projects to "rainy day" personal assistance. Mackinac Associates, the group that supports the activities of the State Park, has grown to over 3,000 supporters and has raised millions of dollars over the years. Its members' generosity has made possible all sorts of improvements to the park, its buildings, and its education programs.

After more than 22 years, my time as a State Park Commissioner came to an end on April 12, 2013. More momentous was the passing, less than a day later, of Grand Hotel's Dan Musser.

Mackinac's "good old days"? Yes, they were good, and they were fun-filled, and they were challenging and certainly never dull. I know from fifty-four years of personal experience.

And I believe Mackinac Island's best days most certainly lie ahead. As for me, I'll always have Rock Fever.

Index of Names

Agnew, James	96
Agnew, Robin Musser	96
Albee, Lynn	20
Allen, Glenn S.	163, 164
Allen, Jason	133, 192
Ames, Hobart	14
Amos, Fran	185
Andress, Bob	41
Andress, Donald (The Duck)	32, 33, 130
Andress, Henry (Chief Eagle Eye)	37, 38, 84
Andrews, Roger	146, 158
Arbib, Roben	16
Armour, Dr. David	149, 156, 157, 159
Arnold, George	195
Arnold, Susan	195
Ballard, Logan	95
Bankard, Rita	66
Barnwell, Becki (McIntire)	73, 130
Barnwell, Sam	213
Barr, John	165
Bazinaw family	36
Bazinaw, Joseph (Snapper)	41
Beardsley, Bill	89
Beebe, Kathryn	163
Benishek, Dr. Dan	192
Benjamin, Bob	69
Benser family	212
Benser, Bob Jr.	193
Benser, Bob Sr.	41
Benser, Gigi	41
Blair, Frank	71
Blanchard, James	26, 101, 137, 139, 141, 142, 146, 151, 157, 182
Bloomfield, Myron Jr.	12
Bloswick, Frank Sr.	105
Bloswick, John Sr.	126, 175
Bouwsma, Oscar	86
Bradley, Elmer (Bud)	127
Bradley, Mike	127
Brodeur, Dennis	16, 35, 41, 53, 69, 120
Brodeur, Leanne	130
Brouwer, Arlie	106
Brown, L. Margaret (Meg)	99, 149, 152, 164, 176
Brown, Marlee (Musser)	99
Brown, Paul	99
Brown, Prentiss family	152, 195
Brown, Prentiss M. Jr.	197
Brown, Prentiss M.	8, 70, 99, 104, 147, 152, 197, 198
Brown, Prentiss M. III	124

Buchman, Dr. Frank	61, 62, 65-67
Bush, George H.W.	26, 30, 36, 137
Cadotte family	36
Cadotte, Eddie	22
Cadotte, Elizabeth	22
Cadotte, Fred (Gunny)	22
Cadreau family	36
Cadreau, Phil (Weenix)	16
Cagney, Jimmy	124
Callewaert family	212
Callewaert, Jennifer	35
Callewaert, Mary	35
Callewaert, Rena	35
Callewaert, Todd	35, 193
Callewaert, Victor	35, 130
Carley, Josh	190
Carley, Mike	130
Caron, Paul	116
Caskey, Charles	95
Caulkins, Henry (Mick)	168
Cawthorne, Brevin	171, 208
Cawthorne, Chase	208
Cawthorne, Cynthia	88, 114, 140, 171
Cawthorne, Kaden	171
Cawthorne, Tyler	171
Chambers family	22, 36, 212
Chambers, "Cannonball Bill"	53
Chambers, Arthur (Bud) Jr.	20
Chambers, Arthur T.	18, 20-21
Chambers, Brad	21, 22, 35, 200, 201
Chambers, Dr. William (Bill)	21, 22, 35, 121, 200, 201, 212
Chambers, Ed	130
Chambers, Jack	14, 19, 20, 35, 41, 49-51, 53,-56, 63-64, 66, 69, 70, 72, 79, 80, 86, 93, 97, 115
Chambers, Jim	20, 21
Chambers, Nancy	35
Chambers, Robert	189
Chambers, Sue	35, 121
Chambers, Terry	41
Chapman, Jimmy	126
Christiansen, Orvin	14
Clinton, Bill	26, 31, 137
Clinton, Hillary	26, 31
Cochran, William	8
Conkey, Brad	184
Cooley, Jim	20
Coolidge, Calvin	25
Cornell, S. Douglas	67
Corrigan family	36
Couchois, Carl	20
Croghan, Maeve	177
Cunningham, Margaret Musser	96, 99
Curtis, Eugene	149
Davenport, Junior	126
Davis, Mildred	119
Davis, Robert W. (Bob)	77, 86
Day, William	74, 76
Dennany, Loretta	92
Deroshia, Louie (The Thief)	33, 35, 106
Deutsch, Stephen	91
Dewey, Dan	190
Dickinson, Luren	51
Dillman, Grover	103

Dodson, Bruce — 186
Donnelly family — 36
Doud family — 36
Doud, Andrew — 213
Doud, Helga — 80
Doud, Jeannette — 205
Doud, Margaret — 35, 68, 77, 186, 188, 201, 204, 205
Doud, Nellie — 124
Doud, Robert — 146, 205
Downing, Neil — 144, 146
Downs, Hugh — 71, 72
Doyle, Catherine — 205
Doyle, Wilfird F.X. (Bill) — 18, 50-53, 62, 64, 66, 86, 104, 135-136, 144-147, 158
Driberg, Tom — 62
Dufina, Dennis — 16
Dufina, Emerson — 73
Dufina, Mary — 41, 117
Dufina, Ron — 35, 41, 93, 117
Dukakis, Michael — 26
Dunnigan, Brian — 181
Dunnigan, James — 53, 66, 90, 144, 146, 149, 166
Durante, Jimmy — 95, 135-136
Early, John and Peter — 172
Early, Michael — 45
Ecker, Sandy — 128
Edwards, Catherine M. — 67
Ellman, William — 158
Emmons, Otto (Bud) — 12, 76, 102, 105
Emmons, Mike — 41
Engler, John — 30, 101, 132, 137, 140, 142, 143, 151-155, 162, 168, 180, 182
Engler, Michelle — 137, 140
Entwistle, Basil — 66-67
Fenlon, Edward — 163
Ferris, Phelps — 145
Ferris, Woodbridge — 145
Ferry, Thomas W. — 145-146
Fischer, Bob — 20
Fitzgerald, Frank — 51, 103, 135
Fitzgerald, John — 9, 163-164
Fitzgerald, Lorabeth — 205
Flanagan family — 36
Flanagan, James Dunleavy (Dun) — 14, 17, 72, 106
Ford, Gerald R. — 26, 29, 137
Ford, Mr. and Mrs. Henry — 62
Foster, Harry — 33, 35, 39
Francis, Cindy — 68
Franks, John — 20
Franks, Mary — 20
Fraser, Hilt — 118
Garrett, Patti — 35
Gast, Harry — 133
Gidley, Mike — 184
Gillespie, Jay — 20
Gillespie, Robert — 20
Gimmel, Dick — 23, 72
Gingrich, Newt — 176
Goodheart, Lenore — 64, 205
Goodman, Benny — 145, 155
Gough, John R. (Jack) — 19, 26, 27
Gough, Taylor — 19

Granholm, Jennifer	138, 143, 153-155, 183-185
Green, Nino	149, 155
Green, Stanley	186
Griffin, Marge	29
Griffin, Robert P.	29
Gunn, Clemens	74, 76
Gustafson, Alice	176-177
Hadden, Frances	125
Hadden, Richard	125
Haggerty, John S.	145
Hammond, Mark	14
Hansz, Jim	20
Harmes, Rollie	180
Harrison, Benjamin	36
Harrison, Michael	15
Haveman, Jim	188
Hayes, Rutherford B.	146
Hayward, Ken	99
Hegarty, Michael	149
Hert, Mrs. Alvin	25
Hinkley, Dana	145
Holden, Creighton	145
Hoppenrath, Kay	130
Horn, Amos	16, 120
Horn, Armand (Smi)	127, 130
Horn, Calvin (Cubby)	186
Horn, Evangeline (Ling)	130
Horn, Nell	120
Horn, Ty	16, 126
Howard, Peter	65-67
Huesdash, Dean	116
Hughey, Robert (Little Bob)	74-75
Hulett, John	30, 99
Humbard, Rex	170
Huthwaite, Bart	33, 168
Jacobetti, Dominic	86, 182
Jaggi, Audrey	150, 155
Johnson, Lady Bird	26, 28
Kelley, Frank J.	66, 101, 124, 137, 145, 149, 150, 152-155, 180, 184, 199, 200
Kelly, Anne	136, 139
Kelly, Brian	136
Kelly, Harry F.	135, 136
Kennedy, John F.	9, 11, 24-25, 36, 137
Kenyon, Frank	103, 156
Keogh, Mrs. Chester	43
King, Stella	130, 188
Kingsley, James	15
Kinney, Stephen	123-124
Knoth, Cynthia (Cawthorne)	88
Krizan, Michelle	123-124
Kughn, Richard	149, 164-165
Lacey, Frances	45-49
Lang, Otto	27, 64, 69, 198
LaPine family	36
LaPine, Carolyn	130
LaPine, Dick	126
LaPine, Robert (Porky)	127
LaPine, Skeezix	37
LaPine, Wilson	126
Lasley, Willard	14
Leeper, Tim	130
Lescoulie, Jack	71
Levy, David	130
Lewand, Kathleen	130, 146, 149, 151, 155, 168

Lewand, Tom	130
Lodge, L. Harvey	86
Lowell, Marshall	29
Mackie, John C.	8
Manoogian, Jane	130-131, 158
Manoogian, Richard	130-131, 150, 155, 173, 174
Marabell, Peter	203
Matheson, Richard	91
Maurer, Wes Jr.	205, 214
Maurer, Wes Sr.	214
May, Harold	55
May, Nancy	209
McCabe, John	124
McCain, John	26
McDowell, Gary	192
McGuire, Barry	69, 71
McIntire, Aaron	73
McIntire, Margaret (Davey)	73
McIntire, Martie	73
McIntire, Mary Kay	73
McIntire, Sam	68, 69, 73
McKillop, Mike	41
McMillin, John	14
McNamara, Kitty	133
McTigue, Pat	155
McVeigh, David	189
Megdall, Tom	20
Michigan Slim	14
Milliken, Bill Jr.	29
Milliken, Mrs. William	29
Milliken, William	29, 50, 52, 88, 101, 136, 141, 171
Moeller, Maria	70, 178
Moore, H. Charles (Charlie)	20, 63, 64
Moskwa, Patti Ann	120
Moskwa, Steve	120
Murdick, Gould	55
Murdick, Newton Jerome	55
Murray family	36
Murray, Walter	53, 144, 146
Musser, Amelia	96-98
Musser, R.D. III	96, 99, 100, 193, 200, 201
Musser, R.D. IV	100
Musser, R.D. Jr. (Dan)	31, 69, 91, 96-99, 100, 191, 200, 201, 214
Myers, Anneke	213
Nelson, Rod	188
Nephew family	212
Nephew, Frank	41
Nold, Carl	149, 158-159
Nordberg, Carl	28, 144, 157
Novak, Stanley	86, 182
O'Brien, Chester	16, 17, 76
O'Brien, Les	16, 24
O'Brien, Ray	79
O'Dell, Sean	35
O'Malley, Charles	36
Orr, Debra	35, 120
Orr, Sandra	35, 120
Osborn, George	8
Osterink, Bruce	155
Palermo, Catherine	16
Palermo, Iggy	16
Pamperin, David	157, 159
Parel, Larry	76
Perault family	36
Perault, Delia	121
Perault, Jim (Sperry)	19, 82

Perault, Sylvia	121	Ryba, Harry	51, 55, 57, 85, 120, 196, 212
Petersen, Dr. Eugene	28, 87, 144, 149, 157-159,	Ryerse, Jim	87
Petersen, Marian	157	Sawyer, Alan	52, 149
Pfeiffelman, Nancy (May)	68	Schlussel, Mark	149, 150, 176
Pfeiffelman, Tom	196, 201	Schmidt, Fred	126
Plummer, Christopher	91	Schmidt, Joseph	163
Porteous, David	154	Schweigert, Thomas	86
Porteous, Joan	150, 154, 155	Seeley, Dan	121, 130
Porter, Bill	158-159, 166	Senn, Larry	41
Porter, Phil	2, 156, 159	Serotkin, David	84
Price, Margaret	145-146	Seymour, Jane	91, 92
Radcliff, Jennifer	163	Shayne, Nathan	69
Raham, Rev. Roland	29	Shepler, Bill	199, 200
Rearick, Doug and Carol	130	Sherman, Mr. and Mrs. Alvin	124
Reeve, Christopher	90-93	Shine, Agnes	23, 83
Rice, Hal	20	Shufelt, John	65, 67, 171, 174, 179
Rich, John T.	145		
Rilenge, Steve	130	Sigler, Kim	52
Roe, Bob	13, 46	**Sink, Charles**	**145**
Romney, George	52, 71, 86, 136, 179, 181	Smietanka, John	153
		Smith, Bill	127
Romney, Lenore	181	Smith, Don (Ducky)	16
Romney, Mitt	26, 153	Smith, Ozro	12
Romney, Scott	153	**Smith, R.J. (Bob)**	**14**
Roosevelt, Franklin D.	25	Smith, Ray	74, 76
Roots, Sheldon	125	Smith, Sheldon	149, 158
Ross, John	115	Snyder, Bob	83
Roussin, Louie	14	Snyder, Rick	153, 155
Rubin, Larry	8	Solomon, Dr. Joe	59, 74, 76
Rudolph, Hugh	27, 70, 198	Squires, Bill	121, 127
Rudolph, Mariana (Nan)	144, 146, 149, 152, 198	Squires, Pat	121
		St. Louis, Lloyd	81
Runkel, Philip E.	162, 163	St. Onge family	36
		St. Onge, Bob	41

St. Onge, Jason	127, 212, 213	Varnum, Charles	86
Staebler, Neil	11	Vernon, F. Dudleigh	20
Staffan, George	41, 171, 174	Visnaw family	36
Stahlin, John	**145**	Vogel, Stephen	149, 150, 152 162
Stamas, Harry	16, 33	Vorce, Mike	20
Steinman, David	8	Walters, Barbara	71, 72
Stockbridge, Francis	94	Wandrie, Otto	186, 187
Stokes, Rod	185	Wandrie, Paul	130
Straus, Lorna	130, 209	Ward, Erica	155
Stupak, Bart	155	Washington, Tom	148, 162, 183
Stupak, Laurie	145, 155	Weeks, George	148, 166
Summerfield, Ray	124	Wellington, Charles	16
Swainson, John B.	52, 71, 136, 147	Wellington, George	16, 127
Swallow, Joe	84, 86	Wessel, Jerry	126
Szwarc, Jeannot	91	White, Peter	145, 146
Tellefson, E.M.	104	Williams, Charlie	30
Teysen, Kenneth	146, 149, 155	Williams, Esther	95, 135, 136
Therrian family	36	Williams, Fr. Jim	155, 156, 212
Therrian, Sonny	82	Williams, G. Mennen	8, 11, 25, 27, 52, 73, 135, 136, 146, 147
Thomson, Len	181		
Thompson, Joseph	144, 146	Williams, Lynn	179
Thurber, Donald	25	Williams, Nancy	25
Timmons, Clayton and Anna	130	Woodfill, W. Stewart	9, 24, 26, 27, 28, 52, 64, 69, 94, 95, 97, 98, 99, 104, 144, 147
Tomlinson, Ron	93		
Traxler, J. Bob	77, 84, 145, 153, 154, 184	Woulfe, Glen	190
		Wynn, Jim	197
Trayser, Mac	209	Yob, Charles (Chuck)	145, 149, 153
Trayser, Tony	69	Young, Lawrence	135
Tremethick, Charles	14	Young, Mike and Wendy	130
Truman, Harry S.	26, 27, 137		
Urman, Gary	133	Yshinski, George	162
VanWagoner, Murray D. (Pat)	8, 18, 34, 52, 62	Ziegler, Hal	84, 87, 88
Varney, Carlton	**97**		

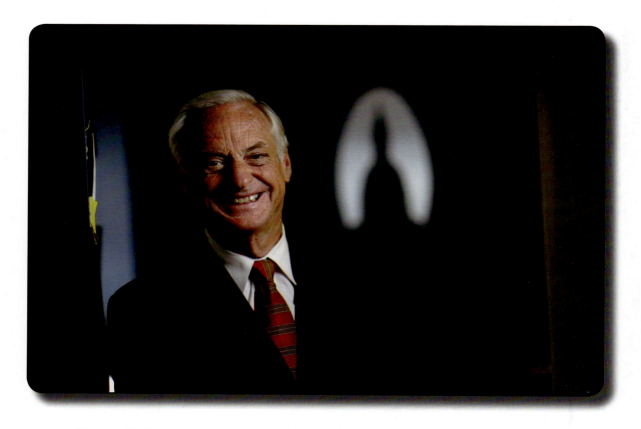

Dennis O. Cawthorne, lawyer, legislator, chairman of the Mackinac Island State Park Commission, businessman, saloonkeeper-restaurateur, chamber of commerce manager, and carriage driver, knows the famed Great Lakes destination, its people, and its idiosyncrasies like few other people. For a great part of each of the last 54 years, he has lived, worked, and played on iconic Mackinac Island.

He is also a world traveler, having visited sixty countries on six continents. He has served as an official United States delegate to international conferences of government leaders in Moscow, Beijing, and Brussels. Mr. Cawthorne is a graduate of Albion College (Phi Beta Kappa) and Harvard Law School.

When not on Mackinac Island or globe-trotting, he makes his home in East Lansing, Michigan. He and his wife Cynthia have two sons and three grandchildren.